YOU CAME UNTO ME
A Training Manual For Jail And Prison Ministry

DEDICATION

This manual is lovingly dedicated to those who inspired it. . .
The women at Central California Women's Facility
and in memory of former death row inmate
Karla Faye Tucker
who went from Texas Death Row safely into the arms of Jesus
on February 3, 1998

Acknowledgments

This manual has been reviewed from several key perspectives:

- An institutional chaplain.
- A death row inmate.
- Religious volunteers ministering inside an institution.
- Volunteers corresponding and visiting one-on-one with inmates.

Special gratitude for assisting in editing portions of the original manuscript to Catherine Thompson, a precious sister in the Lord incarcerated on California's Death Row for Women, and the women of CCWF.   Some forms and content are from The Freedom Fighters Manual by Daniel McManus.

© Harvestime International Network
http://www.harvestime.org

TABLE OF CONTENTS

Introduction 4

Objectives 6

1   "You Came Unto Me": The Biblical Mandate For Ministry 8

2   Qualifications And Preparation 14

3   Starting A Prison Ministry 20

4   Corresponding With Inmates 31

5   Visiting Inmates 35

6   Conducting Group Meetings. 39

7   Ministering To Inmate's Families 47

8   Ministering To Death Row Inmates 52

9   Post-Prison Ministry 57

10   Institutional And Inmate Typology 63

11   Dress And Safety Codes 69

12   Relating To Inmates 74

13   Individualized Guidelines 82

Conclusion: The Word Is Not Bound 83

Appendix One: Dictionary 86
Appendix Two: Scriptures Related To Prisoners 90

Answers To Self-Tests 95

INTRODUCTION

You hold in your hands the key to a great treasure box. Inside the box is gold, silver, and precious jewels. The box in which these treasures are contained is rather unusual--not really very appealing. It is surrounded by razor wire, electrified fences, and armed guard towers. But inside there is great treasure . . . men and women, precious to God, who are waiting for YOU.

The manual you hold in your hands--"*You Came Unto Me*"--is a training guide for jail and prison ministry. This manual provides instruction for every level of involvement:
- The minimal level of corresponding with an inmate.
- Visiting one-on-one with inmates.
- Ministering in group worship services, special programs, or Bible studies inside an institution.
- Assisting inmate's families.
- Providing post-prison ministry upon an inmate's release from a penal institution.

It includes instruction on dress and safety codes, institution and inmate typology, and how to relate to inmates in such a way that they will be attracted to the Gospel message and receive Jesus Christ as their personal Savior.

This manual is designed to be used as a training course for:
- Individuals who have a desire to get involved in jail and prison ministry.
- Churches planning to start jail and prison outreaches.
- Denominations desiring to involve their churches in such ministries.
- Bible colleges desiring to offer jail and prison ministry training to students.
- Chaplains who need a training tool for training their volunteers.

Each chapter includes instructional objectives to guide the learning experience and a self-test to measure individual progress. (Answers to self-tests are provided at the conclusion of the final chapter in this manual and may be removed by the instructor if they do not want students to have access to them.) The Appendices include a dictionary of prison-related terms, Scriptures related to prisoners, and a list of ministry resources.

Chapter Thirteen of this manual is an individualized section where a volunteer, church, Christian organization, or chaplain can insert training materials unique to their specific jail or prison--items like facility maps, rules, dress codes, forms, etc. If you are an instructor using this manual for a Bible college class, you may insert your own lecture notes or handouts in Chapter Thirteen.

You are free to reproduce copies of this manual for the glory of God! The text of the entire manual is available for downloading from the Internet at: **http://www.harvestime.org**

Treasures In Prison Cells
By Bill Yount

It was late at night and I was tired. . .but about midnight, God spoke to me in my spirit and asked a question. . ."Bill, where on earth does man keep his most priceless treasures and valuables?" I said "Lord, usually these treasures like gold, silver, diamonds and precious jewels are kept locked up somewhere out of sight, usually with guards and security to keep them under lock and key."

God spoke. "Like man, My most valuable treasures on earth are also locked up." Then I saw Jesus standing in front of seemingly thousands of prisons and jails. The Lord said, "They have almost been destroyed by the enemy, but these souls have the greatest potential to be used, and to bring forth glory to My name. Tell My people, I am going this hour to the prisons to activate the gifts and callings that lie dormant in these lives that were given before the foundation of the earth. Out from these walls will come forth a spiritual army that will have power to literally kick down the gates of Hell and overcome satanic powers that are holding many of My people bound in My own House.

"Tell My people that great treasure is behind these walls, in these forgotten vessels. My people must come forth and touch these lives, for a mighty anointing will be unleashed upon them for future victory in My kingdom. They must be restored."

Then I saw the Lord step up to the prison doors with a key. One key fit every lock and the gates began to open. I then heard and saw great explosions which sounded like dynamite going off behind the walls. It sounded like all-out spiritual warfare. Jesus turned and said, "Tell My people to go in now and pick up the spoil and rescue them." Jesus then began walking in and touching inmates who were thronging Him. Many, being touched, instantly began to have a golden glow come over them. God spoke to me, "There's the gold!" Others had a silver glow around them. God said, "There's the silver!"

Like slow motion they began to grow into what appeared to be giant knights, armed warriors. They had on the armor of God and every piece was solid and pure gold! Even golden shields! When I saw the golden shields, I heard God say to these warriors, "Now go and take what Satan has taught you and use it against him. Go and pull down the strongholds coming against My Church." The spiritual giants then started stepping over the prison walls with no one to resist them, and they went immediately to the very front line of the battle with the enemy. I saw them walk right past the church, and big-name ministers--known for their power with God--were surpassed by the giant warriors like David going after Goliath! They crossed the enemy's line and started delivering many of God's people from the clutches of Satan while demons trembled and fled out of sight at their presence. No one, not even the Church, seemed to know who these spiritual giants were or where they came from. They were restored to God's House and there was great victory and rejoicing. I also saw silver, precious treasures, and vessels being brought in. Beneath the gold and silver were the people that nobody knew: Rejects of society, street people, the outcasts, the poor and the despised. These were the treasures that were missing from His House.

Then the Lord said. "If My people want to know where they are needed, tell them they are needed in the streets, the hospitals, the missions, and the prisons. When they come there, they will find Me and the next move of My Spirit."

OBJECTIVES

Upon conclusion of this training manual you will be able to:
- Provide references for the scriptural mandate for prison ministry.
- Explain why believers should be involved in prison ministry.
- Articulate the spiritual goals of jail and prison ministry.
- List the social goals of jail and prison ministry.
- Summarize what the Gospel has to offer prison inmates.
- Determine your role in prison ministry.
- Summarize the spiritual qualifications for a prison ministry worker.
- Identify four areas of preparation vital to effective prison ministry.
- Summarize the steps for starting a prison ministry.
- Identify various types of ministries which you might provide in an institution.
- Prepare and submit a proposal for prison ministry.
- Recruit and train volunteers.
- Explain how to get started corresponding with an inmate.
- Summarize guidelines for corresponding with inmates.
- Explain why personal visitation is an important ministry.
- Explain how to get involved in one-on-one visitation with inmates.
- Summarize guidelines for visiting individually with an inmate.
- Identify various group meetings that can be conducted in jails and prisons.
- Summarize guidelines for conducting group meetings.
- Explain why inmates' families are often in crisis.
- Identify ways in which you can minister to inmates' families.
- Summarize guidelines for ministering to inmates' families.
- Explain how to start a ministry to death row inmates.
- Discuss guidelines for ministering to death row inmates.
- Explain how to help a death row inmate prepare to die.
- Identify common needs of ex-offenders.
- Describe types of post-prison ministries.
- List steps for starting a post-prison ministry.
- Determine your role in post-prison ministry.
- Demonstrate understanding of institutional security levels.
- Discuss differences between jails and prisons.
- Discuss common inmate typology.
- Explain how to deal with inmates who maintain their innocence.
- Describe dress codes applicable for all penal institutions.

- Summarize safety codes applicable for all penal institutions.
- Give guidelines for surviving a hostage incident.
- Explain the first rule for relating with inmates.
- Summarize guidelines for relating to inmates.
- Define a "setup," explain how it occurs, and how to avoid it.

CHAPTER ONE
"You Came Unto Me. . ."
The Biblical Mandate For Ministry

KEY VERSE:

. . . I was in prison, and you came to me. (Matthew 25:36)

OBJECTIVES:

Upon conclusion of this lesson you will be able to:

- Provide references for the scriptural mandate for prison ministry.
- Explain why believers should be involved in prison ministry.
- Articulate the spiritual goals of jail and prison ministry.
- List the social goals of jail and prison ministry.
- Summarize what the Gospel has to offer prison inmates.
- Determine your role in prison ministry.

INTRODUCTION

Barbed wire. Steel bars and heavy metal doors. Guard towers with armed officers. Criminals. This is prison!

-Society says, "Lock them up and throw away the key."

-Politicians say, "We need to build more prisons."

-Statistics say, "80% of inmates return to prison after release--we are wasting our time to try to rehabilitate them."

. . . But Jesus says, "I was in prison, and you came to me."

The prison system is the only "business" that succeeds by its failure. Prison populations grow larger and larger. Often, people come out of prison worse than when they went in. Many commit more crimes, return to prison, and get stuck in the cycle of recidivism, the "revolving door" of crime, prison, and release.

The answer to this is not more prisons. It is not locking people up and "throwing away the key."

It is not even the death penalty, as studies have shown that even this does not effectively deter crime. The answer is the Gospel of Jesus Christ in the demonstration of power!

Prisoners need regeneration not rehabilitation--and Jesus has commissioned His followers to reach beyond the barbed wire fences and steel bars to touch the lives of men and women bound by the shackles of sin.

THE MANDATE FOR PRISON MINISTRY

The mandate for prison ministry is clear in God's Word, both by scripture and example.

SCRIPTURE:

The greatest scriptural mandate for prison ministry is given in Matthew 25:31-40. Jesus said:

> . . .**"When the Son of Man comes in His glory, and all the holy angels with Him, then He will sit on the throne of His glory. All the nations will be gathered before Him, and He will separate them one from another, as a shepherd divides his sheep from the goats. And He will set the sheep on His right hand, but the goats on the left. Then the King will say to those on His right hand, `Come, you blessed of My Father, inherit the kingdom prepared for you from the foundation of the world: `for I was hungry and you gave Me food; I was thirsty and you gave Me drink; I was a stranger and you took Me in; `I was naked and you clothed Me; I was sick and you visited Me; I was in prison and you came to Me.'  Then the righteous will answer Him, saying, `Lord, when did we see You hungry and feed You, or thirsty and give You drink? When did we see You a stranger and take You in, or naked and clothe You? Or when did we see You sick, or in prison, and come to You?' And the King will answer and say to them, `Assuredly, I say to you, inasmuch as you did it to one of the least of these My brethren, you did it to Me.'" (Matthew 25:31-40)**

EXAMPLE:

Jesus Christ Himself is our example for prison ministry. One of the main targets of Christ's ministry was prisoners:

> . . . **To open blind eyes, to bring out the prisoners from the prison, and them that sit in darkness out of the prison house. (Isaiah 42:7)**

Jesus declared:

> **"The spirit of the Lord God is upon me; because the Lord hath anointed me**

to preach good tidings unto the meek; he hath sent me to bind up the

**brokenhearted, to proclaim liberty to the captives, and the opening of the
prison to them that are bound". . . (Isaiah 61:1)**

Even while dying on Calvary's cross, Jesus took time to reach out in love and concern to a prisoner. As a result, that convicted criminal experienced God's love, grace, and forgiveness. During the time between His death and resurrection, we are told that Jesus **" . . . went and preached to the spirits in prison" (1 Peter 3:19).**

Unfortunately, despite the clear Biblical injunction and Christ's example to minister to prisoners, many believers prefer to pass by on the other side of the street, as did the religious leaders in the parable of the Good Samaritan (see Luke 10:29-37).

WHY PRISON MINISTRY?

Why must believers be concerned about prison ministry? Because. . .

1. Prison ministry has a direct Scriptural mandate (Matthew 25:31-40). Throughout the Bible are examples, descriptions, and commandments about prisons, prisoners, bondage, captivity, and slavery. The Bible mentions prison, prisoners, or imprisonment more than 130 times. (See Appendix Two of this manual)
2. We should follow the example Christ set by ministering to prisoners.
3. Prisons meet the criteria of any mission field: Lost people and a need for laborers.
4. God is not willing that any should perish--not even serial killers, rapists, and molesters (2 Peter 3:9). God loves even the "worst of sinners" (1 Timothy 1:15).
5. Chaplains cannot minister to more than a small percentage of inmates in their care. They cannot do all of the necessary work themselves, as there is just not enough time to do so.
6. Many jails and prisons have no professional chaplains and many have no religious services at all.
7. For every person incarcerated, there are three to five other people affected: Mates, children, parents, etc. Inmates and their families represent a large segment of society in any culture.
8. False religions and cults are reaching out to prisoners. We must get there first with the Gospel of Jesus Christ!

GOALS OF PRISON MINISTRY

The spiritual goals of jail and prison ministry may include one, some, or all of the following:

-To share the unconditional love of God.
-To present the Gospel of Jesus Christ in such a way that inmates will embrace it and receive Christ as Savior.

-To disciple new believers in the Word and teach them how to study the Bible.
-To demonstrate the power of prayer and teach them to pray.
-To lead inmates to experience the life-changing power of God that will free them from
   guilt, shame, negative emotions, and addictions.
-To minister to inmates' families.
-The social goals of jail and prison ministry are:
-To help the inmate function more positively within the prison environment.
-To provide a link between the community and persons confined in correctional
   institutions
-To prepare residents for re-entry into society (physically, mentally, morally and
   spiritually).
-To assist inmates families in practical ways.
-To provide post-prison assistance in practical ways.

WHAT THE GOSPEL HAS TO OFFER

The Gospel of Jesus Christ has many things to offer inmates.

   -Forgiveness from sin.
   -A chance to say "I'm sorry."
   -Release from guilt and shame.
   -Acceptance--when all many of them have ever known is rejection.
   -New values and perspectives.
   -Strategies for coping with difficult situations and negative emotions
   -Basics for true honest relationships.
   -Life abundant through Jesus Christ.
   -A new purpose for living.
   -Eternal life.

WHAT IS YOUR ROLE?

Of the millions of active believers world-wide, only a small number are involved in ministry to prisoners, despite the fact that jails and prisons are found in almost every community. Yet the scriptural mandate by both teaching and example is clear.

Every believer should be involved in prison ministry. This does not necessarily mean you are called to actually go into a prison. As in missions--not everyone is called to go to a foreign field to share the Gospel. But--as in missions--every believer should be involved in prison ministry in some capacity.

There are many ways to be involved:

-Provide prayer support for prison ministries.
-Visit an inmate.
-Write to a prisoner.
-Assist families of inmates.
-Help inmates transition back to society after their release.
-Conduct worship services, Bible studies, or group meetings inside prisons.
-Write, publish, and distribute Biblically based training material specifically designed for
  prison inmates.
-Provide Bibles and Christian literature for inmates.
-Provide financial support to a prison ministry.
-Serve as a prison chaplain.

Begin now to pray for God to reveal the specific way that you are to be involved!

A New Beginning

"I am a condemned prisoner, sentenced to life without parole--sentenced to die in prison. I have learned that when you feel you have lost everything, God will show that you have gained much more than this world can ever offer.

"Prison is a place where the Lord can shape us into useful tools that can last through a life time of worshiping and praise, whether we are serving six months or a life sentence. The more I study the Bible, the more I long to know more about Christ. . .The longer I stay in prison, the greater my desire to associate with people who live a Godly life and fellowship with them. Prison is where the Lord can do some of His best work.

"Prison does not need to be the end of life. It can be a new beginning--even for one with a life sentence." (R.S.)

SELF TEST FOR CHAPTER ONE

1.	Write the key verse from memory.

____

2.	List the main reference for the scriptural mandate for prison ministry.

____

3.	Who is our greatest Biblical example for prison ministry?

____

4.	List eight reasons why believers should be involved in prison ministry.

___________________________		___________________________

___________________________		___________________________

___________________________		___________________________

___________________________		___________________________

5.	What are the spiritual goals of jail and prison ministry?

____

____

6.	List the social goals of jail and prison ministry.

____

____

7.	Summarize what the Gospel has to offer inmates.

____

____

(Answers to self-tests are given at the conclusion of the final chapter of this manual.)

CHAPTER TWO
Qualifications And Preparation

KEY VERSE:

. . . be an example to the believers in word, in conduct, in love, in spirit, in faith, in purity. (1 Timothy 4:12)

OBJECTIVES:

Upon conclusion of this chapter you will be able to:

- Summarize the spiritual qualifications for a prison ministry worker.
- Identify four areas of preparation vital to effective prison ministry.

INTRODUCTION

Those who minister with inmates must be sure of their relationship with Christ, set a proper example, and always be ready to give an answer for the hope within them. While a person called to this ministry should demonstrate all the spiritual virtues taught in the Word, this chapter emphasizes the essential qualifications prison workers should possess:

SPIRITUAL QUALIFICATIONS

COURAGE:

Entering a jail or prison to minister--whether on a one-to-one or group basis--is outside the "comfort zone" for most believers. It is not unusual to feel a bit uneasy the first few times you are in a penal facility---but remember, God will take care of you whenever you are in His service. In most cases, the prison chapel is a safe place and inmates are open and friendly. If you feel apprehensive, remember that God does not give a spirit of fear--so recognize where fear comes from and conquer it in the name of Jesus!

COOPERATION:

There are many different persons in a prison society. As a volunteer--in addition to the inmates-- you will primarily be involved with correctional officers (also called guards) and a chaplain or supervisor. Most people you meet will probably treat you with courtesy and respect. Be sure to treat them courteously, speaking to them and shaking hands with them where appropriate, using their names when reasonably possible. A good prison worker knows how to cooperate with others--administration, other volunteers, and especially the chaplain, if the jail or prison has one.

It is important for you, as a volunteer, to have some understanding of the work of jail and prison chaplains. Chaplains work long hours under difficult conditions. Each day chaplains must deal with many responsibilities such as the personal crises of inmates, providing programs to meet the spiritual needs of inmates, and fighting the frustrations and disappointments which are an integral part of prison chaplaincy.

Most full-time prison and jail chaplains have more training and preparation for their work than do many ministers. Before they can be accepted into many prisons they must have seminary training and be endorsed by their denominations. Often they are required to have served in a pastorate before coming into chaplaincy. Chaplains must also be acceptable to the warden of the prison in which he/she is to work.

A chaplain functions as the administrator of a religious program for the entire institution. He/she provides for the traditional preaching and worship functions, oversees religious education programs; spends much time in personal counseling; recruits, trains and supervises volunteers; and performs many administrative activities (letters, meetings, reports.)

It is important for volunteers to maintain good relationships with the chaplain. It is a grave breach of trust to use your access to the prison to undermine the chaplain's reputation or to discredit his programs. If there is a problem, always talk with the chaplain first.

GENUINENESS:

Be real! Inmates are adept at identifying phonies. A person should not visit the prison with an improper motive like seeking a spouse or showing off his/her abilities. Prisoners are extremely perceptive. They can quickly spot the person who joined the team out of curiosity. Selfish motives and "holier-than-thou" attitudes have no place in this ministry.

HUMILITY:

Maintain a humble spirit. Remember--you are there to serve. Always be in subjection to those in authority (the chaplain, guards, warden).

FORGIVING:

Foster a forgiving spirit, recognizing that but for the grace of God, you could be in a similar situation. Realize that God's forgiveness extends to what society calls "psychopaths" and the "vilest of individuals."

PERSEVERANCE:

Society, friends, and family have given up on many inmates. They don't need someone else to reject them. Be patient. God has promised you will reap spiritual fruit in due season. Volunteers who start and then quit demoralize the inmate, disappoint the chaplain and the prison staff, and give a bad image to the efforts of the church.

FAITHFULNESS:

Be faithful, constant, and trustworthy in the performance of your duties, especially in keeping promises and being on time for appointments or services. The prison chaplain depends on you, as do the inmates. A visit that may just be another in a long list of things you have to do can be the highlight of an inmate's week. Don't disappoint them. Be faithful to this great privilege with which God has entrusted you. Commitment to be consistent and dependable is a top ranking quality valued by chaplains who work with volunteers.

EMPATHY:

Empathy is the ability to feel with people as though you were in their place. In the Old Testament, the Prophet Ezekiel sat with the captives by the River Chebar before he shared God's message to them. They were ready to listen, because they knew he understood. He had "sat where they sat" (Ezekiel 1:1).

SENSE OF MISSION:

A sense of mission is a desire and determination to give this work priority (at the times designated for it), a belief that this is what you would rather be doing (at that time) than anything else in the world!

SPIRITUAL GROWTH:

You must not only lead inmates to new spiritual growth, but likewise you must be willing and anxious to grow. Spiritual growth is a lifelong process. If you ever feel that you have "arrived" in either knowledge or virtue, you are simply showing how immature you really are.

EMOTIONAL MATURITY:

It is important that you can handle your own emotions: Anger, depression, up one day and down the next. Prison is a depressing place and inmates don't need more gloom and doom.

LOVE:

Study 1 Corinthians 13. The greatest motivating force behind any ministry--and especially prison ministry--is love. Love for God. Unconditional love for the inmate. Love for the mission to which God has called you.

PREPARATION

There are four vital areas of preparation for those who desire to be effective prison workers.

1.   **PREPARE IN PRAYER:**

As in every ministry, effective prison ministry is fueled by prayer. Here are some specific prayer targets:

> -The chaplain of the institution.
> -Individual inmates.
> -Families of inmates.
> -The warden and administrative staff.
> -Correction officers.
> -Safety for prison volunteers entering the institution.
> -Parolees: For their spiritual and practical needs--jobs, housing.
> -Revelation knowledge to meet the needs of inmates.
> -Spiritual revival.
> -For God to raise up strong spiritual leaders within the prison church body.
> -Inmate prayer requests: Many prison chapels have a prayer request box. Inmates write out their requests and put them in the box for the chaplain and volunteers to pray specifically for their concerns.

2.   **PREPARE IN THE WORD:**

The prison volunteer should have a good working knowledge of the Bible and basic Christianity. Most inmates are not interested in the finer points of theology, but they do need a clear, understandable presentation of the gospel. If you do not study and understand the Word, how can you help someone else learn to study and understand it? To be an effective prison worker, you must continually be studying God's Word.

3.   **PREPARE FOR YOUR SPECIFIC RESPONSIBILITY:**

Prepare for your specific responsibility in ministry. If you are to sing, have your sound track cued and ready. If you are to teach, spend adequate time preparing your lesson. If you are using video or audio equipment or an overhead projector, have these items ready.

4.   PREPARE FOR THE SPECIFIC INSTITUTION:

Prepare yourself for the specific institutional setting you will enter:

-Know the rules for dress and conduct of the specific institution. These vary from institution to institution.
-Know the chain of command--who you are responsible to as a volunteer.
-Know what you are allowed to take into the institution with you.
-Get a general understanding of the ways in which acceptable Christian ministries can be carried out within that system.
-Attend training and orientation classes offered by the institution or chaplain.

The Lady Behind The Walls
By Kassie Logan

At times it is a lonely place,
No loved ones to be found,
A search for inner happiness,
Yet depression keeps you bound
As I sit and look outside the fence,
At the traffic passing by,
The amazement of it all,
Makes me stop and question "Why?"
Why has the Lord bestowed on me,
Such an awesome cross to bear?
Why would the loving God I serve,
Allow something so unfair?
Time to me is nothing new,
Must accept as best I can,
For I know that in the scheme of things,
My Jesus has a plan.
And someday, out those gates I'll walk,
When the Lord's voice gently calls,
And I will tell my story,
About "the lady behind the walls."

SELF-TEST FOR CHAPTER TWO

1.   Write the key verse from memory.

____

____

2.   Summarize the spiritual qualifications for a prison ministry worker which were discussed in this chapter.

____

____

____

____

____

____

3.   Identify four areas of preparation vital to effective prison ministry.

____

____

____

____

(Answers to self-tests are provided at the conclusion of the final chapter of this manual.)

CHAPTER THREE
Starting A Prison Ministry

KEY VERSE:

But this is a people robbed and plundered; all of them are snared in holes, and they are hidden in prison houses; they are for prey, and no one delivers; for plunder, and no one says, "Restore!" (Isaiah 42:22)

OBJECTIVES:

Upon conclusion of this chapter you will be able to:

- Summarize the steps for starting a prison ministry.
- Identify various types of ministries which you might provide in an institution.
- Prepare and submit a proposal for prison ministry.
- Recruit and train volunteers.

INTRODUCTION

You are convinced. The Biblical mandate and example are clear. As a believer, you want to be involved in prison ministry. But how do you start? How do you gain access to the prison? This chapter details steps for starting a jail or prison ministry. You will learn various types of ministries which you might provide in an institution, how to prepare and submit a proposal for your program, and ways to recruit and train volunteers.

STARTING A JAIL OR PRISON MINISTRY

Here are seven steps to guide you through the process of starting a jail or prison ministry.

STEP ONE: Pray

All things are fueled by prayer. Pray about what God wants for the specific institution and your individual role in it. Lay a foundation of prayer before you begin your ministry.

STEP TWO: Consult your spiritual leader

If you are a pastor, consult with your board. If you are a church member, talk with your pastor. This is important for several reasons:
-It is common courtesy.
-Spiritual leaders can guide and provide valuable input to you.

-Your spiritual leader may already have plans underway for such a ministry. If so, be
part of it, don't undermine it.

Try to gain the interest and support of your pastor or spiritual leader. This support is vital to
obtaining volunteers to staff the program. The key will be in showing your pastor how this
ministry works cooperatively with other programs, ministries, and services of the church.   Share
how this scripturally mandated outreach advances the Gospel by putting church members to work
both inside and outside institutions.

STEP THREE: Do an analysis

Here are some questions to answer in your analysis:

-What jails and prisons are in your immediate area?

-Is there a local ministerial association? What are they doing, if anything? Are they interested in
jail and prison ministry? (If they already have a program and have gained access to local
institutions, perhaps you can be part of it.)

-Who is in charge of volunteers at the institution? Contact them and find out:

-How do you get cleared for ministry inside the institution.
     -Are there forms you need to fill out?
     -Is there special training you must take?
     -What identification do you need for clearance?

-What needs exist in their institution?

    -What needs can you and/or your church fill? Try not to duplicate efforts of other
Christian organizations. We should complement, not compete with one another.

    -Familiarize yourself with all the rehabilitation programs offered in local institutions
where you wish to serve, as well as the population breakdown (races, religions, ages, sex,
etc.) and, if possible, the philosophy of the respective administrations. Gain as much
knowledge as you can about the institution before requesting permission to provide
services and/or programs. If you know administrators, officers, or former inmates, talk to
them about the needs and conditions.

-Possible activities and services you can provide an institution include:
        -Conducting regular church services.
        -Substituting for the chaplain when he is ill or on vacation.
        -Providing special musical or dramatic programs.
        -Conducting Bible studies.
        -Teaching classes in a specific skill, trade, or in personal adjustment.
        -Conducting a Christian group for those with addictions.
        -Distributing literature and Bibles.
        -Hosting a Christian film night.
        -Providing individualized services in addition to your group program:
                -Providing Bible correspondence courses.
                -Matching inmates with Christian visitors.
                -Matching inmates with Christians to write to them.
                -Providing referral information for families of prisoners.
                -Referring inmates to post-prison release programs.

Note: Before writing this portion of the ministry proposal, you may want to study Chapters Four-Nine of this manual which address various individual and group ministries in which you may desire to become involved.

STEP FOUR: Prepare a program proposal

A proposal will . . .

        -Define purpose, objectives, and practical aspects of your program.
        -Be submitted for approval to the institution where you plan to minister.
        -Be used as a tool for volunteer recruitment. (You must know what type of ministry you will be conducting in order to recruit qualified volunteers.)

Your proposal should consider things like. . .

Goals: What is the purpose of your program? What do you want to accomplish? See Chapter One of this manual for a list of possible goals. Be sure to include your own specific goals also.

Benefits: How will your program benefit inmates? How will it benefit the institution?

Specifics: Define the specific ministry? Will it be a group ministry? To individual inmates? Their Families? A post-prison ministry?

Director: Who will head your program? What are his/her qualifications and experience?

Volunteers: Who will participate in your program? What training will they receive? (We suggest using this manual in your training program. That is the purpose for which it was created.)

Facilities: What type of facility will you need at the institution? Do you need to use the prison chapel? A day room? A classroom? A visiting area?

Days, time: Days and times you would like to meet.

Equipment: Will you need items like an overhead projector, video projector, musical instruments, song books, musical sound tracks? Are these items provided by the institution or will you need to provide them? Will the institution allow you to bring them into the facility? If you plan to prepare handouts for inmates, do you have access to a copy machine?

Funding: Although most group prison ministries are operated by volunteers, there may be financial costs incurred--for instance, if you plan on distributing Bibles, books, tracks, or other handouts approved by the institution.

The institution in which you plan to minister may have a special form or format to follow in preparing your proposal. Inquire concerning this. Following is a sample proposal form used by one prison in the United States:

Sample Proposal Form

1. Who will your program be directed towards?
2. Who will have responsibility for your program?
3. What are the objectives of your program?
4. What services does your program offer to inmates?
5. What services does your program offer to the Institution?
6. What specific format will be used to present your program ?
7. What type of theological training/ credentialing/ prison program experience does the
primary facilitator have?
8. What is the detailed itinerary for your program?
9. What days/hours will your program meet?
10. How many people are involved in your program?
11. How will they be trained?
12. How large an area would you require for your meetings?

The following information is required to do a background investigation on each person you plan to bring into the institution:
     1) Name
     2) Date of Birth
     3) Driver's License number
     4) Social Security number

Please provide us with references regarding your past prison involvement and/or any other information that characterizes the uniqueness of your ministry.

Following is a sample letter format used for a proposal to an institution:

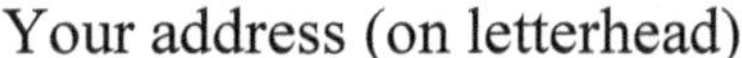

Your address (on letterhead)

Date
Their address

Dear

We are requesting permission to conduct a prison ministry program at the (Name of institution).

Our program will be directed to the inmate population, but we believe it will also benefit the institutional staff by providing inmates with an opportunity for better use of free time and improvement in inmate morale. It has also been demonstrated that inmates who become true adherents of what the Bible teaches make good citizens of a correctional environment. Their influence positively affects other prisoners and causes them to respect authority and to avoid situations that cause tensions and hostilities between staff and inmates.

Our volunteers will be trained in a prison ministry training course, wherein we will acquaint them with dress and safety codes, institutional and inmate typology, and how to relate to inmates. In our training, emphasis is placed on knowing and enforcing rules and avoiding possible risks to security. Of course, should it be necessary, we shall be pleased to go through any required orientation provided by your staff.

At this time, we are prepared to offer any part or all of the following services: (Describe in detail the program you plan to offer, using the guidelines given in this chapter).

In the near future, I look forward to talking with you concerning the details of this proposal. Thank you for your time and all consideration given to this request.

Respectfully submitted,
(Your name)

If you have already successfully conducted prison ministries elsewhere, attach letters of recommendation and/or commendation from jail or prison officials at the institutions where you ministered. If you have received requests from inmates in the institution for the specific program you are offering, attach these to your proposal.

STEP FIVE: Submit your proposal

Submit a copy of your proposal to your pastor or spiritual leader for review, then submit a copy to the chaplain or proper authorities at the prison and wait for their response. They may call you in to meet with them to discuss the proposal. If so, be on time, appropriately dressed, and properly prepared for your appointment. If you do not receive a response to the proposal after a reasonable length of time, take the initiative to call and schedule an appointment yourself with the person to whom it was submitted.

If your request to provide services is denied, try again in a couple of months. This could very well be a test of your commitment, dedication, and patience. Administrators and chaplains also quit, retire, or transfer and someone else may be more favorable to your program.

> *Note: At present, in the United States it is the responsibility of the institution's administrator to ensure that all residents are able to exercise their constitutional right to practice their religious beliefs. The only way this right can be denied is that substantial justification can be shown to limit or regulate it, (for example, a security breach).*

STEP SIX: Secure and train volunteers

After approval of the prison ministry by your pastor and the institution in which you plan to minister, you need to secure volunteers to conduct the program. A volunteer is important. . .

-To the inmate, as a link to the outside world, a friend, and a model of mature Christian life.
-To families of inmates, in providing information and practical and spiritual help as they cope with their dilemma.
-To the chaplain, by assisting and supporting his programs.
-To the prison administration, as an additional resource for helping with rehabilitation and transition back into society. The volunteer can provide services the institution cannot provide because of limited staffing and budget.
-To other volunteers, as a source of encouragement, training, and example to follow.
-To the local church, as a channel of communication, increasing awareness of the need for jail and prison ministries.
-To himself, as this ministry provides an opportunity for using his spiritual gifts and putting his faith into action.

There are many ways to obtain volunteers:

      -Put a notice in church bulletins.
      -Make announcement in church services.
      -Recruit at small group meetings.

-Prepare posters and place them in strategic locations in the church.
-Plan a "Prison Ministry Day" in the church or churches you plan to involve in the ministry. Have a speaker who is actively involved in prison ministry and include testimonies from former prisoners. Outline the program you plan and announce a meeting (date, time, place) for those who are interested in participating. (In addition to recruiting volunteers, the "Prison Ministry Day" will prepare churches to receive former prisoners into their fellowship.)

In screening volunteers, consider the following:

-Has the person had prior prison ministry experience?
-Does the person have any musical talent?
-What languages do they speak?
-Do they have the ability to lead a small group?
-Have they had any personal witnessing experience?
-What is their spiritual gift? Teaching and counseling are two important gifts for jail and prison ministry.
-Are they an ex-offender? If so, check to be sure they will be allowed access to the prison.
-Determine where their interest lies and where they will be most effective:
-Writing an inmate?
-Visiting an inmate?
-Ministry to inmate's families?
-Group ministry inside the prison?
-Post-prison ministry?

You may want to have each potential volunteer complete a form at the first meeting. Use the following form or make your own adaptation of it:

Questionnaire For Volunteers

(All information to be kept in strict confidence)

Name____ Age_________ Sex_______

Address:____

City__________________ State or Province__________ Postal

Code____________________

Home Phone (_____)_______________ Marital Status: ___Single ___Married

Occupation & Title_____________________ Work Phone (___)_______________

Member of what church? _________________Located at:_____________________

Please check the area(s) of prison work that you are most interested in. If you check more than one, please number your selections according to preference.

___Correspondence/letter writing   ___Group Bible studies
___Providing transportation   ___Worship service
___Follow-up with ex-prisoner   ___Follow-up with family
___Writing to an inmate   ___Visiting an inmate one-on-one

Have you ever been arrested? If "yes," list date(s), place(s), charge(s) and disposition(s).

____

Have you ever been in a mental institution?_________ If "yes," when and how long?

____

Do you have to take medication for any reason?_________ If "yes," please explain:

____

Do you have any experience working with a prisoner(s)?_________ If "yes," please explain:

____

What languages do you speak?

____

Do you play a musical instrument or sing? If "yes," what?_______________________

Circle group you are interested in: Males   Females   Juveniles

Signature_____________________________________ Date_______________

Note: If women are allowed on the volunteer team for a men's institution, it is important to remember that the highest standards of conduct and dress should be insisted upon. The same is true for men ministering in women's prisons. When possible, have husband and wife teams. These teams not only prevent difficult situations arising, they add the extra dimension of modeling good husband-wife relationships.

After you secure your volunteers, train them:

-Review your prison ministry proposal with them.
-Discuss where they would fit best in the program.
-Use this manual to train them for jail and prison ministry.
-Arrange for some orientation to the institution as a first step in developing interest and eliminating those who feel uncomfortable with this type of ministry.
-Be sure to obtain proper clearances to enter the institution for volunteers.
-Have your volunteers complete any training required by the chaplain or the administration of the institution in which you will be ministering.

STEP SEVEN: Plan your first meeting or outreach

-Be sure volunteers are well trained.
-Be sure everyone is dressed properly for visitation or group outreach at the prison.
-Check that everyone has the proper identification for entering the facility.
-There are many different ways a service or group meeting inside the prison can be run. If you discover an effective format, don't hesitate to make it the backbone of your ministry--but don't be afraid to try new ideas and fresh approaches from time to time. See Chapter Six of this manual for guidelines for conducting prison services.
-Be certain everyone clearly understands their individual role in the ministry: What to do, when, and any time constraints involved.

"Keep reaching out to people inside prisons. There are many people in here like me who love the Lord--or who could be like me--people in whose lives they could make a difference if they will reach out to them. If the Church would see them and embrace them as part of the Body of Christ--disciple and nurture them in the Lord and teach them to disciple others around them--a revival will break out inside these walls."

-Texas Death Row Inmate
-Karla Faye Tucker
-February 3, 1998

1.   Write the key verse from memory:

____

____

2.   Summarize the steps for starting a prison ministry discussed in this chapter.

____

____

____

3.   What are some various types of ministries which you might provide in an institution?

____

____

____

4.   What are some ways to recruit volunteers?

____

____

____

5.   What were some suggestions given in this chapter for training volunteers?

____

____

____

(Answers to self-tests are provided at the conclusion of the final chapter of this manual.)

CHAPTER FOUR
Corresponding With Inmates

KEY VERSE:

These things I have written to you who believe in the name of the Son of God, that you may know that you have eternal life, and that you may continue to believe in the name of the Son of God. (1 John 5:13)

OBJECTIVES:

Upon completion of this chapter you will be able to:

- Explain how to get started corresponding with an inmate.
- Summarize guidelines for corresponding with inmates.

INTRODUCTION

This chapter is for those who wish to be involved in a correspondence ministry with jail or prison inmates. It explains how to get started and presents guidelines for safe and effective correspondence.

HOW TO GET STARTED

First, contact the proper authorities at the institution. Some prisons provide programs that match inmates to "friends outside" for corresponding and/or visits. If the prison does not have such a program, contact the chaplain for names of those who need someone to write to them.

Second, obtain a list of the rules for corresponding with inmates at that specific prison. Most institutions have established, written rules that govern correspondence.   These differ from institution to institution. Some prisons permit you to send stamps and stationary through the mail, soft cover books, Gospel tracts, Bibles, and cassette tapes. Other institutions have specific procedures for sending such materials, i.e., the book must come directly from the publisher. Some institutions do not permit inmates to receive any of these items through the mail.

GUIDELINES FOR CORRESPONDING

Here are some guidelines to help you correspond effectively with inmates.

1.   Keep in mind as you write to prisoners that many of them feel suspicious, resentful, and lonely.

-They are suspicious, because they have been abused or taken advantage of in past relationships. They may question your motive for writing: "What are you getting out of doing this?" Work at developing mutual trust, respect and understanding.

-Inmates are often resentful because they have been rejected by society, and after all, you too are a member of that society.   Give inmates unconditional love and understanding.

-Inmates feel lonely because they are alienated from society, friends, and family. Many have been rejected by the latter. A week without a letter can seem like a year, so write often and respond promptly. One prisoner is reported to have called mail "paper sunshine."

2. Pray that God will help you to properly understand each letter and direct you with the proper response. (See Chapter Twelve on "Relating To Inmates").

3. If possible, it is best not to use your home address when answering letters. Use a post office box or your church or ministry address. This will avoid possible future problems, i.e., another inmate getting your home address, a parolee showing up unexpectedly on your door step, etc.

4. Make it clear from the beginning that you are not looking for romantic involvement.   It is easy for prisoners to become infatuated, even if they have never seen you, because of their loneliness.   Kindness from you can be misinterpreted by them. If this happens, you should straighten it out in your very next letter or visit. Be courteous and tactful, but firm in this area. Some ministries restrict pen-pals to the same sex.

5. Do not share anything about yourself that can be used against you later, for any reason.

6. Do not send money unless you have really prayed about it and know God is directing you to do so.   If you do send money, never loan it. Send it as an outright gift, but make it clear not to expect future gifts. Be sure to clear the gift through proper channels at the institution.

7. Do not promise help with employment, housing, etc., after release from prison unless the ministry with which you are involved is adequately prepared to give it. Your purpose in writing is to be a source of encouragement in the Lord. Any request for social services should be channeled to proper post-prison release ministries.

8. Do not be too "preachy" in your letters. Establish relationship first, then it is easy to share regarding spiritual matters. Share incidents from your everyday life that make the inmate feel part of your life and family.

9.   Include in your letter anything you are permitted to send such as. . .
        -Photos.
        -Interesting news clippings.
        ~Crossword or word search puzzles.
        -Picture post cards.
        -A gift of stamps or stationery, from time to time, if the institution permits.
        -Funny cartoons.
        -Paper book marks.
        -Bible studies or correspondence lessons.

"It is so overwhelming--the letters I have received--there is nothing to
describe it. I am so blessed. Thank you, from the depth of my being. There
are no words to express what it means. My heart cries out that others can
experience it also."
                        -Texas Death Row Inmate
                        -Karla Faye Tucker
                        -(regarding her correspondents)

1.   Write the key verse from memory.

____

____

2.   What are important things to do when you want to get started corresponding with an inmate?

____

____

3.   Summarize the guidelines for corresponding with inmates discussed in this chapter.

____

____

____

____

____

(Answers to self-tests are provided at the conclusion of the final chapter of this manual.)

CHAPTER FIVE
Visiting Inmates

KEY VERSE:

Remember the prisoners as if chained with them--those who are mistreated--since you yourselves are in the body also. (Hebrews 13:3)

OBJECTIVES:

- Explain why personal visitation is an important ministry.
- Explain how to get involved in one-on-one visitation with inmates.
- Summarize guidelines for visiting individually with an inmate.

INTRODUCTION

Many inmates in jails and prisons have no one to visit them:

> -Their family may live a great distance from where they are incarcerated or do not have the necessary transportation/finances to visit.
> -Their family may have rejected them or they may have no family.
> -Former friends may have rejected them.

Personal visits with an inmate is one of the most rewarding areas of jail and prison ministry. This chapter explains its importance, details how to get involved, and offers guidelines for visiting individually with inmates.

THE IMPORTANCE OF PERSONAL VISITATION

Visiting an inmate on a one-on-one basis is an important ministry for the following reasons:

-Every soul is valuable to God: "The Lord is not willing that any should perish" (2 Peter 3:9). Jesus ministered to multitudes, but He always had time for the individual (for an example, see John 4).

-Many inmates will not attend religious services. Perhaps they have been "turned off" to the church by negative experiences. They may also be afraid going to prison services will be interpreted as weakness by other inmates and make them vulnerable.

-Many inmates have never experienced true, Godly, unconditional friendship. They have only known abusive or impure relationships.

-As for most of us--it is easier to open up in a personal rather than group setting. You can discuss many issues in a one-on-one visit that you cannot discuss in a group setting. The inmate can share personal needs with you, you can pray and study the Word together, and forge an intimate spiritual bond.

-You become a bridge back into society for the inmate. They will have a friend waiting when they are released from prison.

-One can't have too many friends. You will not only be a blessing, but you will be blessed by a true friendship with an inmate.

HOW TO GET INVOLVED

Here are some guidelines for how to get involved in one-on-one visitation with inmates.

-Inquire about the visitation program at the jail or prison where you want to volunteer. Many have an organized program for matching inmates with volunteers who want to visit one-on-one.

-If the institution does not have an organized program for matching inmates and visitors, ask the chaplain to match you with an inmate. If there is no chaplain, consult the administrator in charge of visiting and ask for a match.

-People who are ministering inside the prison on a group basis in religious programs are also a good source. They often know of inmates who have no one to visit them or who would benefit from personal attention.

-If possible, exchange a few letters with the inmate prior to your first visit. You will already feel like friends when you meet for the first time.

VISITATION GUIDELINES

Here are some visitation guidelines:

-Go through proper channels to be approved by the institution as a visitor. You may have to fill out certain forms, be pre-approved before your first visit, carry a specific type of identification, etc.

-Learn and abide by all rules for personal visitation in the institution where you are to visit. Rules may include issues like days and hours for visitation, appropriate dress, safety, and dress codes.

They usually govern what can and cannot be taken into the institution with you.   Many jails and prisons have their rules in writing. Ask for them. (For general guidelines, see Chapter Eleven of this manual on "Dress and Safety Codes.")

-It is best to visit one-on-one with a person of your same sex. This avoids the pitfalls of improper romantic relationships.

-Normally, it is best not to give money to an inmate or their family. If you believe there is a legitimate need and you really believe God is directing you to do this, it is best to channel your help anonymously through the chaplain or another contact in the institution.

-If you forge a real friendship with an inmate it will be easier to discuss spiritual matters and share the Gospel with them.

-Don't preach or lecture. Ask God to show you how to share His love and the Word of God in a way that will be accepted. After an inmate becomes a believer, continue to disciple him in the Word of God.

-If the institution permits, give a Bible and discipleship literature to your friend. Depending on institutional rules, you may be allowed to send these items through the mail, take them in yourself, or give materials to the chaplain to deliver.

-Unless you have had training or you are gifted by God in the area of personal counseling, don't assume this role in the relationship.   You are there as a friend. Don't feel you must give an answer to every issue raised.

-As in any friendship, be a good confidant. Keep personal information shared by your special friend confidential.

-Prison is a very impersonal, dehumanizing place and an inmate doesn't have much opportunity to receive individual attention.   Make your friend feel special. Make your visits a positive, uplifting, fun time.

-Always remember you are there as a representative of the Lord Jesus Christ--but don't spend all your time on spiritual matters. Foster a balanced relationship just as you do with your own personal friends. Discuss current events, laugh together, have fun with your friend!

1. Write the key verse from memory.

____

____

2. Why is personal visitation an important ministry?

____

____

3. List ways to get involved in one-on-one visitation with inmates.

____

____

____

4. Summarize the guidelines given in this chapter for visiting individually with an inmate.

____

____

____

____

(Answers to self-tests are provided at the conclusion of the final chapter in this manual.)

CHAPTER SIX
Conducting Group Meetings

KEY VERSE:

But when He saw the multitudes, He was moved with compassion for them, because they were weary and scattered, like sheep having no shepherd. (Matthew 9:36)

OBJECTIVES:

Upon conclusion of this chapter you will be able to:

- Identify various types of group meetings that can be conducted in jails and prisons.
- Summarize guidelines for conducting group meetings.

INTRODUCTION

Many jails and prisons offer opportunities for group ministries to inmates. This chapter identifies various types of group ministries and suggested guidelines for conducting the groups.

TYPES OF GROUP MEETINGS

There are many types of Christian group meetings to conduct in a prison:

```
-Worship services
-Bible studies
-Music classes  (to train vocalists, musicians, or a choir for the prison worship services)
-Musical and dramatic presentations
-Christian writing
-Small groups offering a Christian approach to addiction and/or emotional problems
-Parenting classes
-Bible college courses
-Discipleship classes for new believers
```

Remember to follow the guidelines given in Chapter Three of this manual for preparing and submitting your proposal to the institution.

CONDUCTING GROUP MEETINGS

Here are some general guidelines for conducting group services in a jail or prison.

TIMING:

Correctional institutions are run on a strict schedule. All group meetings should begin and end on time.

MUSIC:

Music for worship services in prison should be encouraging and uplifting. Songs that could be misunderstood by residents as condemning or as "put down" should not be used, e.g., "Rescue the Perishing." Neither should depressing music like "Nobody Knows The Trouble I've Seen."   If you are using overheads transparencies, song books, or sound tracks, have these items ready. Always receive clearance from the chaplain before arranging musical activities which are different from that which your team normally does (special groups, cantatas, etc.)

PRAYER:

Here are some suggestions for prayer time:

> -Keep prayers short and to the point unless the Holy Spirit moves in a special way. A lengthy prayer could not only make the worship tedious but could be misunderstood by the prisoners as saying, "These people need long prayers."

> -No particular position or posture is important, but when there is a large crowd (50 or more), it would be advisable to leave the congregation seated or standing while offering prayer rather than calling them forward to kneel. (This is for control purposes.)

> -Spend most of the time praying for the physical, social, mental and spiritual welfare of inmates--their concerns and those relating to their families. Pray also for institutional staff.

> -It is okay to keep your eyes open a bit (or have a member of your team designated to keep their eyes open) for control purposes.

SCRIPTURE READING:

The person reading the Scripture, during a worship service, is "echoing" the voice of God and setting the tone for the sermon or lesson. Have the text read with expression, reverence and impressiveness (see Nehemiah 8:8). Announce clearly, before beginning to read, where the Scripture is located (book, chapter and verses). Allow time for those who have Bibles to find the passage. Project your voice to those in the back of the room. Stand erect and speak clearly. Read

God's Word so impressively that the prisoners' emotions will be stirred and their hearts turned heavenward.

TESTIMONIES:

If you are asked to give a testimony, do not view this as your golden opportunity to preach. Do not use denominational jargon such as, "Since I came into the message" or "After I accepted the truth." It is better to use such phrases as "Since I became a Christian" or "After I accepted Jesus Christ as my personal Savior."

Keep your testimony Christ-centered and follow the ABC's of testifying:

A.   Always tell what Christ has done for you and/or your family, telling things that are relevant to strengthening the faith of the prisoners. Don't glamorize sin by telling explicit details.

B.   Be sure to keep it as short as possible, preferably 2-3 minutes. Don't try to tell it all. Remember that you are working in a scheduled time frame. The more you talk, the less time the speaker will have to deliver the Word.

C.   Check your volume. Speak clearly and loudly, especially if no microphone is available, so you are heard and understood by all.

PREACHING OR TEACHING:

Messages prepared for preaching or teaching in a prison should not exceed 30 minutes (unless, of course, the Holy Spirit is moving in some dramatic way). Many inmates have limited attention span. You also want to leave time enough at the end of your message so that you can conclude things properly and visit awhile with the residents (the fellowship is important to them).

Make your messages relevant to inmates. Adjust your presentation to what you know about your audience. Character building and encouragement messages are always good. When making a point about wrongdoing, always use "we" to include yourself.

The following things should **never** be done in a message:

-Never scold the residents. Enough of this has been received from relatives, lawyers, judges, etc.
-Never make statements that can be misinterpreted by prison staff as a breach of security.
-Never downgrade other religions.
-Never present a "holier than thou" attitude.
-Never ask antagonistic questions or assume the group disagrees with you.

-In small groups, wherever possible, use the circle seating arrangement.
-In small groups, encourage class participation. The question and answer method is effective. Don't let one person dominate the conversation.
-Make sure everyone has a Bible and encourage them to read along.
-If you have to eject a disruptive student from a group, be tactful and courteous, but be firm. If necessary, get the cooperation of a correctional officer.

RESPONSE:

If you ask for response from the group at the end of a message--to accept Christ as Savior or rededicate their lives--be very clear about exactly what you want them to do and why. If you have a large group, it is best to have them raise their hands rather than come forward (security precautions).

INMATE PARTICIPATION:

Encourage inmates to be part of the service. For example, have an inmate sing a solo or share his testimony. Exercise caution with regard to the content and length of inmate participation. Keep in mind that you are working within a set time frame and you can allow only a minimum amount of resident participation at each service. If necessary, have a "waiting list." Be sure to screen solos inmates want to sing, as some who are new believers may not pick appropriate music. Always maintain control. Do not let any inmate take control of the group meeting.

In small group meetings--especially Christian groups dealing with addictions--provide opportunity for all inmates to participate and share. You may be jarred by one inmate verbally attacking another in such sessions. Intervene by directing the group back to issues rather than dealing in personalities.

FOLLOW-UP:

Inmates who indicate their acceptance of Jesus Christ as their personal Savior during an appeal at the close of a group meeting--or at any other time--should receive follow up care while still in the institution.

If possible, their names should be secured and one copy given to the chaplain and another retained for you to follow up. Encourage them to attend Bible study sessions, Sunday services, and other opportunities offered in the institution.

If the institution provides a way for them to be baptized in water, they should receive instruction on this and opportunity to do so. (One prison has a horse watering trough which the chaplain fills with water for baptismal services.)

New converts will be like young children taking their first spiritual steps. Most of the time, their environment will be alien and opposed to their new beliefs. Constant support, encouragement and prayer is needed. They should:

-Be kept as spiritually active as possible by participating in worship services, Bible studies, and other Christian activities.

-Be given some responsibility in the ministry as soon as they are ready to accept it. Many are quite talented and their appropriate talents should be utilized for God's service. A study of spiritual gifts will help them identify and begin to flow in the gifts God has given to them.

-Be encouraged to continue regular attendance at worship services and Bible study sessions.

Be encouraged to develop friendships with other Christians within and without the institution. You may want to assign a "spiritual buddy" to each new convert. This person will visit and/or write the resident regularly, as well as keep in touch after his/her release from prison.   If the prisoner with whom you are working is transferred to another institution, the "spiritual buddy" can continue to write and provide encouragement and spiritual guidance. (Caution: Be sure the "spiritual buddy" is the same sex as the convert.)

ENTERING AND EXITING THE ROOM:

It is important--especially in large groups--to have established procedures for entering and exiting the room to keep things orderly. Some institutions require inmates to sign in so there is a record of their participation.   Assign some inmates to remain behind and put the room back in order: Erase boards, secure equipment, put up materials, pick up trash, and straighten chairs and tables.

A Journey To The Harvest Field

The Approach: You can see the lights from ten miles away, illumined against the western backdrop of a glorious sunset. The road we travel is lined on one side with fig, peach, and nut trees which are now yielding their rich annual harvest. On the other side of the road the combines are harvesting hay. But ahead of us . . . where the lights burn in the distance . . . is the greatest harvest.

The Entry: As we drive onto the prison grounds, we first pass a guard post with numerous warning signs:
> -You are entering a restricted area: No weapons, guns, knives, or drugs.
> -You are required to consent for search of your person and belongings.
> -You are entering an area with known AIDS infection.
> -In the event of a prison riot, we have a policy of non-negotiation for hostages.

First we enter the visitors center. There we must remove all jewelry, any items in our pockets, our belts, and watches. A search is made of our Bible and book bag and we pass through the metal detector. We are then logged in, given a badge, and our arms are stamped with an ultraviolet identification code. We exit the visitors center to a small cubicle and wait for the large gate to slide open. When it does, we step inside another small cubicle. The gate behind us clangs shut with a loud crash, then the gate in front of us opens and we proceed on to the control center. At the control center, we ring the outside bell. The gate is opened, closes behind us, our identification is checked, and another large door opens. At last . . . we are inside the main yard of the prison facility. We are surrounded by tall fences topped with razor wire. We cross the grounds to a small room on the east end where the harvest awaits.

The Harvest: Simple wooden chairs fill a plain, rectangular room. There are no stained glass windows, no carpet, or comfortable pews. But the room is packed with the harvest of human lives. Women fill the chairs, line the walls, and sit on the floor.

-Let us introduce you first to AG, who is serving 15 to life for killing a drug pusher. Her life has been miraculously changed by the power of God. She is personally responsible for many other "lifers" who fill the classroom. They came to have their own lives changed when they saw the difference in her life.

-SK was a teacher until that fateful night when she drank too much, got into her car, and struck and killed a pedestrian. SK is now a born-again Christian.

-DL came from a background of Satanic worship. She was a high priestess in the church of Satan. As a child, she was abused by her step-father and had her first child at age 12. Serving time for kidnapping and drug related offenses, she has been saved, filled with the Holy Spirit, and obtained her college degree from a Christian university while incarcerated.

-AM came from drugs and prostitution. She never completed anything in her life that she started until she finished a course in the prison Bible college. She is paroling tomorrow, and tonight she stands with radiant face to give glory to God. She walked in these gates alone. She walks out with God

We wish we had time to introduce you to each one of the students. They are former thieves, addicts, embezzlers, prostitutes, and murderers. What education, rehabilitation, and counseling could not do, the power of the Gospel has done. As we minister the Word of God, you will see tears of repentance. You will hear voices lifted in praise to God. You may even see dancing and shouting before the Lord. Although they are still behind bars and rows of razor wire fences, these women have found freedom in Jesus Christ. This is the true harvest.

SELF-TEST FOR CHAPTER SIX

1.   Write the key verse from memory.

____

____

2.   List various types of group meetings that can be conducted in jails and prisons.

____

____

3.   Summarize guidelines given in this chapter for each of the following areas:

Timing____

____

Music____

____

Prayer____

____

Scripture reading____

____

Testimonies____

____

Preaching or teaching____

____

Response____

____

Inmate participation____

____

Follow up____

____

Entering and exiting the room_____________________________________

____

(Answers to self-tests are provided at the conclusion of the final chapter of this manual.)

CHAPTER SEVEN
Ministering To Inmate's Families

KEY VERSE:

". . .and in you all the families of the earth shall be blessed." (Genesis 12:3)

OBJECTIVES:

Upon conclusion of this chapter you will be able to:

- Explain why inmate's families are often in crisis.
- Identify ways in which you can minister to inmate's families.
- Summarize guidelines for ministering to inmate's families.

INTRODUCTION

Thousands of families are directly affected each year by having one of their loved ones in a prison or jail. Most of these families are broken and filled with loneliness, anxiety, and feelings of rejection. Few of these families receive adequate attention from the church.

God told Abraham that through him, "all the families of the earth shall be blessed." As spiritual heirs of Abraham, we too can bless families. This chapter explores ways you and/or your church can be involved in ministering to the families of inmates.

UNDERSTANDING THE CRISIS

When a family member is arrested, it usually creates great anxiety, fear, and uncertainty for their mate, children, or parents. Imprisonment brings a double crisis to a family. The first crisis is that one of the family members has been arrested for breaking some law. The second crisis is that the family is split apart. Losing a family member to imprisonment is similar to the person dying.

Children face shame and loss when a parent is in prison. They may be displaced, having to live with relatives, friends, foster homes, or in institutions. Many do not get to visit the incarcerated parent--perhaps because of court orders, distance from the prison, or the financial situation of those keeping them which prohibits visiting (costs for transportation, food, housing).

HOW TO HELP INMATE'S FAMILIES

Here are some practical ways to minister to inmate's families:

Transportation and hospitality: Provide transportation to and from the institution so the family can visit. If you live near a prison, provide a place for the family to stay overnight while visiting. Studies have shown that a family that stays together and keeps in touch with the member in prison have an important influence in helping that member readjust to society upon release.

Information: The family may not know how to get information--things like trial dates, when and how to visit, or how to obtain legal representation. You can be a help if you familiarize yourself with the system.

Social services: Share information on public and private agencies whose function is to provide employment, legal aid, housing, financial assistance, counseling, education, etc. The family may also need assistance in applying for these programs.

Employment: If the wage earner is incarcerated, the mate may need to find employment.

Housing, food, clothing, and finances: The family may need temporary or permanent housing, food, or finances to help get them on their feet. If you or your church provides financial help, checks should be used--if possible--and made out for the bills involved, directly to the landlord, utility companies, etc.

Counseling: The entire family or individual family members may need personal counseling in order to deal with the crisis.

Presents on special occasions: Christmas and birthdays are difficult for children and their incarcerated parent(s). One way you can help is to purchase gifts for Christmas and birthdays, wrap them, and present them to the child from the incarcerated parent. This cheers both inmate and child!

A church home: The most important thing you can do for an inmate's family is to provide a loving, supportive, accepting church home.

HOW TO CONTACT AN INMATE'S FAMILY

There are two important things you must do before contacting an inmate's family:

-Check with the chaplain or administration at the jail or prison where you are ministering. See if there are rules against this or an established procedure you should follow.

-Obtain written permission from the inmate so the family and institution knows you have his/her approval.   The request also clarifies the purpose for your contact. You may use and/or adapt the following form.

Family Contact Request Sheet

We are happy to follow up your request for us to contact your family members in order to provide encouragement, counseling, Bible studies, and practical needs when possible--but we need your permission. Please complete this form. Please print:

Name____

Inmate identification number____________________ Dorm Information___________________

Institution_______________________________ Location___________________________________

Please contact:

Name Of Family Member	**Address**	**Telephone**	**Relation To You**	**Purpose For Which You Want Us To Contact Them**

____

____

Signature_______________________________________ Date_______________________

Approval by institutional chaplain or administrator:

By_________________________________   __________
      Signature   Date

A friendly telephone call or brief visit should initiate this ministry. At the culmination of the visit or call, offer a brief prayer. On the next visit, bring a copy of the same literature that the inmate is using for adult family members so they can progress spiritually together. If they are not interested in the literature, then continue visiting on a strictly friendly and supportive basis. Always try to channel the conversation towards the present conditions of the home, family, employment, and plans for the future. Discourage attempts to dwell on negative aspects of the past. On subsequent visits, the family may share personal problems with you. If a basic need is obvious, tactfully inquire if you may be of assistance in filling it.

Note: Husband and wife teams are ideal visitors. Men should never visit an inmate's wife alone, nor should a woman visit an inmate's husband alone.

When you are working with an inmate's family, keep all personal matters confidential.   Share only that which you have received specific permission from the incarcerated family member to reveal. Never get involved in legal matters or mention alleged problems between the prisoner and his/her family.

Inside A Russian Prison. . .
A Challenge For International Prison Ministries
By Patricia Hulsey

As we enter the prison, long, dark hallways with crumbling plaster and rusting pipes lead to even darker stairwells. We descend the stairs and cross a frozen yard with vicious guard dogs barking from behind their enclosures. We then enter the hallway of a damp cell block lined with heavy metal doors.

Crowded cells with fifteen prisoners and five beds are not uncommon. The inmates sleep in shifts because of lack of beds. Many beds lack sheets, blankets, or mattresses. There are no personal hygiene products. There is no privacy for the one toilet facility in the room. A dim electric bulb hangs from the ceiling. The stench is horrible. There is no fresh air. There are no televisions, radios, or books. There are no religious services. Inmates shower once a week and are only allowed out of the cells fifteen minutes a day. The cells are infested with lice. Lunch is a green looking broth served in tin bowls.

It was into these dismal surroundings that we went from cell to cell ministering the love of Jesus, distributing Bibles and study materials. Just before the heavy metal doors clanged shut behind us, one inmate--a spokesman for that cell block--commented, *"We thank you for the things you have brought us, but what is more important is that you cared to come at all."*

1.   Write the key verse from memory.

____

____

2.   Why is an inmate's family often in crisis?

____

____

3.   What are some ways in which you can minister to inmate's families?

____

____

____

4.   What are two important things you must do before contacting an inmate's family?

____

____

5.   Summarize guidelines given in this chapter for ministering to inmate's families.

____

____

____

____

(Answers to self-tests are provided at the conclusion of the final chapter in this manual.)

CHAPTER EIGHT
Ministering To Death Row Inmates

KEY VERSE:

Let the sighing of the prisoner come before thee; according to the greatness of thy power preserve thou those that are appointed to die. (Psalms 79:11)

OBJECTIVES:

Upon conclusion of this chapter you will be able to:

- Explain how to start a ministry to death row inmates.
- Discuss guidelines for ministering to death row inmates.
- Explain how to help a death row inmate prepare to die.

INTRODUCTION

Some prisons have "death rows"--special units where prisoners are housed who have been condemned to death by the legal system of their nation, state, or province. These inmates are usually kept in segregated or maximum security facilities. Death row is a unique segment of the penal institution, and this chapter is designed to help you minister effectively in this environment.

HOW TO START A MINISTRY TO DEATH ROW INMATES

A ministry on death row--as any prison ministry--must be approved by the chaplain or administration of the institution. In most instances you will not immediately be allowed access to a death row. A chaplain or administrator will want to observe you in other settings in the prison-- in group or individual ministry to general population inmates.

Some institutions do not allow group ministries on death row because of the security risks. Don't be discouraged--you may be allowed to minister on a one-on-one basis through visiting or writing a death row inmate. This can be very effective, both in terms of fostering genuine relationships and sharing the Gospel message. It may also lead to the possibility of group ministry later on.

If group meetings are not allowed, explore alternative ways of ministering on death row. For example, in one institution where group ministry was not permitted a video player was approved to be taken in and the chaplain and volunteer ministries supplied Christian videos to the row. Some modern institutions have closed circuit television capabilities and perhaps these could be used to air video-taped services. Christian audio tapes may also be permitted. You may also be able to match each death row inmate with a Christian visitor who will minister one-on-one to them.

<h2 style="text-align:center">MINISTERING TO DEATH ROW INMATES</h2>

If you are ministering by writing or visiting one-on-one with a death row inmate, review Chapters Four and Five of this manual for guidelines on writing and visiting. If you are conducting group ministry, see Chapters Six, Eleven, and Twelve. The general guidelines in these chapters are applicable to death row also.

Unique to death row are the following guidelines:

-There are sometimes different rules for visiting, writing, or conducting group services on death row because of security issues. Inquire about these regulations and abide by them religiously!

-If a death row inmate maintains innocence, it is not your place to challenge it. There are many instances where inmates have been released from death row after it was proven without doubt that they were innocent. If they maintain their innocence, pray with them that God will undertake and justice be done.

-Feelings of isolation, depression, and hopelessness are very common because death row inmates are usually segregated, confined more often to their cells, and very limited in options as to what prison programs they can participate in. You can help by being an uplifting friend and providing ways to fill their time (puzzles, games, arts and crafts, reading material, correspondence courses, etc.--whatever is permitted by the institution).

-People are usually sentenced to death row because of the violent nature of the crimes of which they have been accused and convicted. Some may admit their guilt, but not show any remorse for their crime. You must have the ability to accept them just as they are and then--through love and the life changing power of God--lead them to the place they need to be.

-You must have a real understanding of Biblical regeneration: ". . .if anyone is in Christ, he is a new creation; old things have passed away; behold, all things have become new" (2 Corinthians 5:17). Society may still require the inmate to pay for his crimes with his life, but God has forgiven him/her and they are a new creation. They are not the same person who did the crime.

-Be sure the death row inmate understands that turning to God does not necessarily mean He will deliver them from death. Share Hebrews 11 with them. Many godly people were delivered from death, but others were killed. Some were delivered out of prison; others were not. God wants to give them dying faith as well as living faith.

-Continue to hold on in faith with a death row inmate until all legal appeal options have been exhausted--but then don't be afraid to help him prepare if death is eminent.

Is there someone they need to forgive? Guide them in the process.

-Are there those to whom he needs to apologize and seek forgiveness— victims, their families, his own family or friends? Guide them in the process.

-If they have young children, encourage them to write a special letter to the child to be given to them when they are older.

-Do they have any practical business matters that need to be concluded?

-Discuss death openly, and the fact that as a believer, there is nothing to fear. Everyone has an appointed time to die. The only difference between them and other believers is, they know their date. This can be a positive thing, for it gives them time to do and say what needs to be said and done. For the believer, death is swallowed up in victory:

> **Behold, I tell you a mystery: We shall not all sleep, but we shall all be changed--in a moment, in the twinkling of an eye, at the last trumpet. For the trumpet will sound, and the dead will be raised incorruptible, and we shall be changed. For this corruptible must put on incorruption, and this mortal must put on immortality. So when this corruptible has put on incorruption, and this mortal has put on immortality, then shall be brought to pass the saying that is written: "Death is swallowed up in victory. O Death, where is your sting? O Hades, where is your victory?" (1 Corinthians 15:51-55)**

Death releases us from the sins, trials, and burdens of this life:

> **For we know that if our earthly house, this tent, is destroyed, we have a building from God, a house not made with hands, eternal in the heavens. For in this we groan, earnestly desiring to be clothed with our habitation which is from heaven, if indeed, having been clothed, we shall not be found naked. For we who are in this tent groan, being burdened, not because we want to be unclothed, but further clothed, that mortality may be swallowed up by life. (2 Corinthians 5:1-4)**

When a believer dies, it is precious in God's sight:

Precious in the sight of the LORD is the death of His saints. (Psalm 116:15)

At death, the believer immediately enters the presence of the Lord.

We are confident, yes, well pleased rather to be absent from the body and to be present with the Lord. (2 Corinthians 5:8)

-Help them focus on eternity and the tremendous things that await in Heaven. See Revelation chapters 21 and 22.

If a death row inmates asks you to be present at their death to provide spiritual support, do so if the prison permits it. You can help make it a glorious home coming instead of a frightful experience--for truly, the death row inmate who has become a new creature in Christ will go right from that death chamber into the presence of God!

**[There Are No Door Knobs Here
By Catherine Thompson
California Death Row For Women**

"I have been approached several times by friends and associates to put my thoughts on paper. Until recently, I shunned the idea. But a few days ago an outsider looking into our unit asked how I handle being on death row and facing the state possibly taking my life. Another individual asked if I was okay because I never complain and always have a smile.

"What no one realizes is that I had my last true smile on June 13, 1990. The next day, my best friend, my confidant, and the love of my life was taken from me by a very violent crime. That was the last day I can truthfully say I felt sincere happiness and exhibited a true smile. Through this experience I have learned what I call the daily three Ps of my existence: Patience, perseverance, and purity. I take one day at a time and there are some days I have to take one hour at a time.

"There are things I took for granted all my life that I now consider a privilege, such as a phone call, going out for sun and fresh air, or even simple things like turning a door knob or opening a window. There are no door knobs here. My door is electronically controlled by a correctional officer from a control booth.

"As a productive citizen of society, I voted against the death penalty. I feel God has numbered all our days on earth and does not give man the authority to change that. No one--be it a criminal or society--has the right to murder. I sit and wait on the state to appoint an attorney to represent me on appeal because I cannot afford to buy justice. In our society, justice--as everything else-- comes with a large price tag.

"In the meantime, I spend my days upholding my dignity. My freedom was taken, my heart was broken, my smile destroyed--but no man can take my dignity."

1.   Write the key verse from memory:

____

____

2.   Summarize the suggestions given in this chapter on how to start a death row ministry.

____

____

____

____

3.   Discuss the guidelines given in this chapter for ministering to death row inmates.

____

____

____

____

4.   Discuss the suggestions given in this chapter for helping a death row inmate face death.

____

____

____

(Answers to self-tests are provided at the conclusion of the final chapter in this manual.)

CHAPTER NINE
Post-Prison Ministry

KEY VERSE:

> **...To open blind eyes, *to bring out the prisoners from the prison*, and them that sit in darkness out of the prison house. (Isaiah 42:7)**

OBJECTIVES:

- Identify common needs of ex-offenders.
- Describe types of post-prison ministries.
- List steps for starting a post-prison ministry.
- Determine your role in post-prison ministry.

INTRODUCTION

Some prisoners are released after serving their entire sentence as prescribed by law. In some legal jurisdictions, after completing part of their sentence, prisoners are eligible to go before a parole board. If granted parole before finishing their sentence, they are released with certain conditions, such as reporting regularly, not associating with ex-felons, and restrictions governing living and working arrangements. Conditions for release vary and are usually set by the court, a parole board, or a parole officer.

Inmates being released from prison have many needs as they reenter society. This chapter will help you identify these needs, understand various types of post-prison ministries, and define your role in ministering to ex-offenders.

THE NEEDS OF THE EX-OFFENDER

Some inmates are blessed to be returning to supportive families or churches upon release from prison, but if they do not have such a support network then post-prison ministry is very important. Each person is different and has unique needs, but here are some common needs most ex-offenders share upon discharge from an institution.

>   -He needs to be accepted in a local church that is nurturing and supportive so he can develop spiritually. Invite him/her to go to church with you. Sit with them and invite them to have a meal or snack with you after service.

-He needs housing, food, and clothing. Inmates who have no "street clothes" sometimes need a "parole box"--a box containing clothes, underwear, and shoes that he can wear when he leaves the institution grounds.

-He needs vocational training and/or a job.

-He may need financial counseling (basics of budgeting, maintaining personal finances, etc.) **A special note:** Don't give financial help personally to an ex-offender. It is better that financial assistance be channeled through your church or the administrators of a post-prison program.

-Family counseling is important if he is trying to reunite his family.

-He may need additional personal counseling for addictions like drugs and alcohol. Believers who have made a commitment to Christ may find addictive temptations one of their first spiritual battles on the outside.

-If he has been incarcerated for a long time, he may need assistance with even simple decisions because inmates have very limited options for making decisions in prison.

-He needs a strong support network of friends who will love and accept him, pray for and with him, and help him work through problems.

In addition, find out as much as possible about the inmate before release. This knowledge will assist in post-prison ministry. Determine his job skills and educational level. Find out where he is paroling to (sometimes it is required that an inmate go to a certain geographic location). Discuss plans with the chaplain and the appropriate institution authorities before you speak to the inmate about it. Do not promise anything if you cannot follow through on it.

POST-PRISON MINISTRIES

There are different types of post-prison ministries which you may want to start and/or to which an inmate can be referred:

-**A Christian "half way house."** This is a group home for ex-offenders and is called "half-way" because it is a transition between prison and getting back into normal society. This type of ministry usually provides housing, food, counseling, and job placement assistance to its residents. Participants may remain there for a set time dictated by authorities or until they find employment and housing. Some group homes have a discipleship program and participants are required to complete the program before moving out on their own. If you start a half-way house, it is important that you have strict rules concerning drugs, alcohol, curfews, and other general behavior standards.

-The local rescue mission: Some cities operate rescue missions that accept ex-offenders into their discipleship and vocational programs.

-Government or privately operated programs: Some areas have government or privately operated programs to help ex-offenders be integrated back into society. These may include group homes, vocational counseling, and other assistance.

-Church based programs: A local church may choose to start an ex-offenders group, offering assistance in housing, counseling, and job placement. Business owners in the church may be recruited to give an ex-felon a job. One church opened a fast-food restaurant that was run entirely by born-again ex-felons.

-Christian colleges and Bible schools: Some offer scholarships, room, and board to promising ex-felons. If you are an administrator of a Christian college or Bible school, this would be a tremendous post-prison ministry to offer.

STARTING A POST PRISON MINISTRY

Here are five steps for starting a post-prison ministry:

STEP ONE: Pray

All things are fueled by prayer. Pray about what God would have you do in the area of post-prison ministries.

STEP TWO: Consult your spiritual leader

If you are a pastor, consult with your board. If you are a church member, talk with your pastor. This is important for several reasons:
    -It is common courtesy.
    -Spiritual leaders can guide and provide valuable input to you.
    -Your spiritual leader may already have plans underway for such a ministry.
     If so, be part of it, don't undermine it.

STEP THREE: Do an analysis

Here are some questions to answer in your analysis:

-Are there any local post-prison ministries? If so, what are they? (You may want to become part of a post-prison ministry already in existence.)

-What needs exist in your community in regards to post-prison resources?

-What needs can you and/or your church fill? (Try not to duplicate efforts of other Christian organizations. We should complement, not compete with one another.)

STEP FOUR: Visit a similar ministry

If you decide to start a post-prison ministry, visit a similar ministry that exists elsewhere. Learn from their successes and failures.

STEP FIVE: Determine organizational issues

Here are some organizational issues to determine:

-**Funding:** Post-prison ministries need financial resources. Determine how funds will be secured and develop an operating budget.

-**Facilities:** What type of facility is needed? Where will it be located? Can you get required approvals by the local government to locate the facility in the area you are considering?

-**Staffing:** Who will run the post-prison ministry? What are the necessary qualifications? Will the positions be paid or volunteer?

DETERMINING YOUR ROLE

What will your role be in post-prison ministry? It depends on the answer to the following questions:

1. What is permitted by the institution in which you minister? Some institutions prohibit volunteers who minister inside the prison from working with inmates after their release. They reason that should the inmate return to prison, they might be too familiar with the volunteer or be shown special favors because of their relationship outside the institution.

2. Where are you most effective? Are you more effective ministering to inmates inside or upon release from prison?   Where does your interest and vision lie? Which gives you the greatest joy and the greatest spiritual results?

3. What are your time and energy limitations? You can't be everything to everyone. Due to personal time and energy restraints, you may need to confine yourself to ministering to inmates either inside or upon release, but not both.

If your institution does not permit your involvement with inmates upon release or you do not have the time or burden for post-prison ministries, then you will want to serve only as a referral agent. Make a list of churches, individuals, or para-church organizations involved in post-prison ministries and refer inmates to them.

Whatever your involvement, your role should be that of a friend and facilitator. Don't become a crutch for the inmate. Be available, but don't smother him/her. Encourage self-reliance.

SELF-TEST FOR CHAPTER NINE

1. Write the key verse from memory.

    ____

    ____

2. What are some of the common needs of ex-offenders discussed in this chapter?

    ____

    ____

    ____

    ____

3. List some types of post-prison ministries.

    ____

    ____

4. List the steps for starting a post-prison ministry.

    ____

    ____

5. What three questions should determine your role in post-prison ministry?

    ____

    ____

    ____

(Answers to self-tests are provided at the conclusion of the final chapter in this manual.)

CHAPTER TEN
Institutional And Inmate Typology

KEY VERSE:

The spirit of the Lord God is upon me; because the Lord hath anointed me to preach good tidings unto the meek; he hath sent me to bind up the brokenhearted, to proclaim liberty to the captives, and the opening of the prison to them that are bound. . . (Isaiah 61:1)

OBJECTIVES:

Upon conclusion of this chapter you will be able to:

- Demonstrate understanding of institutional security levels.
- Discuss differences between jails, prisons, and other facilities.
- Discuss common inmate typology.
- Explain how to deal with inmates who maintain their innocence.

INTRODUCTION

Are some inmates considered more dangerous than others? Are there any differences between a jail and a prison? Do inmates share any common characteristics? How do you respond to someone who maintains their innocence? These are key issues that are addressed in this chapter.

INSTITUTIONAL TYPOLOGY

Each jail and prison is unique, but most institutions are classified by the type of inmates they house:

> **-Maximum security institutions**: These house inmates that are the greatest risk, perhaps due to the nature of their crime or their behavior in prison. Death rows are usually located in maximum security institutions. These inmates have very close supervision and their participation in institutional programs run by volunteers is sometimes restricted.

-**Medium security institutions**:   These are less violent inmates who do not pose a great security or escape risk. They do not require as much supervision and may be allowed to freely participate in religious programs.

-**Minimum security institutions**:   These are composed of inmates who are close to their release date, incarcerated for non-violent crimes, or those who have proven themselves to be extremely reliable and trustworthy. They may even work outside the prison on occasion and usually have freedom to participate in religious programs.

Some institutions house all three security levels in various areas of the same facility. Each of these levels are often found in jails also. Institutions sometimes clothe the inmates in uniforms of differing colors to identify the various security levels.

DIFFERENCES BETWEEN JAILS AND PRISONS

Although jails and prisons both house offenders, there are differences between the two. Prison inmates have been tried and convicted.   Jail is usually the entry point for all prisoners. Many jail inmates haven't been convicted of anything yet. Most are being held pending trial. Some are being held pending sentencing. Some may be serving sentences so brief that it doesn't warrant sending them to a prison.

Prison population is relatively stable. People serve longer terms so you have more time to work with them. Jail population is very transient. People are held in jails only while awaiting trial, sentencing, or serving brief sentences. Your time with them is limited.

Some prisons have at least a minimum of facilities and programs for counseling and rehabilitation, but most jails have few or none. Prisons usually have better facilities for group meetings such as church services and group Bible studies.

The physical, emotional, and psychological conditions of jail inmates are different from and less favorable than those in prisons. There is usually no privacy in which to talk with individual inmates in jails.   The prisoners in jails are often bored, restless, and fearful. Most of all, uncertainty rules their lives.

OTHER TYPES OF FACILITIES

Other types of programs of confinement include:

-**Work release centers:**   Allow an inmate to hold a job in the community during the day and return to the center for confinement at night.

-Halfway house: For persons on parole. They are required to stay at the house while seeking employment and a permanent place to live. They may be required to complete certain counseling or training programs offered at the halfway house.

-Road camp, fire camp, forestry camp, or work farm: Inmates work on roads, fight fires, or work on public forests or a farm.

-Detention, juvenile hall, or reformatory: Typically for young offenders to be kept separate from older prisoners.

Despite the distracting environment, jails, prisons, and other penal programs are some of the greatest spiritual harvest fields in the world. Jesus only had a few minutes with the dying thief on the cross, but his entire destiny was changed for all eternity.

INMATE TYPOLOGY

Each inmate is unique. God loves each one and is not willing that any should perish. There is no "typical" inmate in God's sight, but there are some common characteristics that will help you understand the majority.

Education: Often, the educational level of inmates is low.

Home environment: Inmates often come from homes where there was abuse, divorce, little supervision, and no discipline.

Vocational training: Many inmates have little or no vocational training. They may have been unsuccessful at obtaining or maintaining employment or labored at low paying jobs.

Self-image: Inmates often have low self-image because they have been rejected by society, friends, or family.

Emotional profile: Many inmates suffer from guilt over what they have done or put their families through. Depression, hopelessness, and hostility are common.

Social responsibility: Inmates sometimes have a limited sense of social responsibility. They may feel no remorse for their crime or that they got a "bad break" from the system by coming to prison.

Common Offenses: Four crimes account for the majority of prison inmates in most countries: Robbery, burglary, murder, and narcotics violations.   Other common reasons for incarceration are sexual offenses, kidnapping, assault, embezzlement, forgery, and fraud.

Inmates also assume various roles in prison that you should be aware of in ministry:

> -**"Hecklers"** may come to a Bible class as earnest students and then disrupt by asking unanswerable questions. They may try to pour out scandalous stories about the church and ministers or turn testimony time into a gripe session. Maintain control of group sessions by continually bringing the group back to the subject at hand.

> -**Perennial seekers** respond to every altar call due to a lack of understanding of what conversion is all about, a desire to please you, or because they have lived like a sinner since they last responded. Continue to receive them warmly when they respond and pray with them. When they are secure in their relationship with God and really understand conversion, they will change.

> -**Manipulators** are those who may be charming and agreeable, but try to use you to accomplish their own purposes. Review "How To Avoid A Setup" in Chapter Eleven of this manual for suggestions in how to deal with them.

> -**Institutionalized** inmates are those who have been confined for a lengthy period of time and have difficulty functioning apart from an institutional setting. If they return to prison after paroling, don't be discouraged. They may be sincere in their confession of the Lord but just need more skills for adjusting to life outside.

Remember--these characteristics are not true of all inmates. Some are very educated and held high paying jobs. Some came from good homes and supportive families. Some are sincere seekers, desiring to learn about God. These general characteristics are based on numerous studies of the majority of prison inmates.

Most important, remember to view each inmate not as they were, or even as they are. View them as the valiant men and women of God that they will become when the Gospel has supernaturally impacted their lives!

ARE SOME REALLY INNOCENT?

Many inmates maintain their innocence. For some who are actually guilty, this can be an escape mechanism. They cannot face what they did, so they rationalize or blame others. ***But please--be aware--some inmates who maintain their innocence actually are innocent!*** There have been many cases where inmates were released from prison after it was proven--beyond a doubt--that they were wrongly convicted. (This applies to former death row inmates also!)

You are not there to judge the guilt or innocence of an inmate. You are there to be a friend and minister God's love to them. Be supportive. Tell them you will pray for God to undertake in their case and for justice to be done.

Remember that--for various reasons--many heroes of the faith ended up with prison records.
Joseph spent at least two years in prison after he was falsely accused of attempted rape (Genesis
39). Samson was imprisoned by the Philistines (Judges 16). Jeremiah was put into King
Zedekiah's dungeon twice, once for unpopular preaching and once when falsely accused of
treason (Jeremiah 32,37).

Many of the apostles were thrown into prison by the Sadducees (Acts 5). Herod imprisoned John
the Baptist (Matthew 4) and Peter (Acts 12), as well as Paul. The apostle Paul had a lengthy
prison record. He served sentences in Jerusalem (Acts 23), in Caesarea (Acts 23), a local jail in
Philippi (Acts 16), and probably two different times in a prison in Rome.

Christians have been imprisoned throughout church history--John Bunyan and Dietrich
Bonhoeffer are two most notable believers who were incarcerated. Modern China, Russia, and
Uganda have seen thousands of believers imprisoned and martyred.

Jesus said that being a faithful Christian may lead to prison (Matthew 10 and 24). Conversely,
being a prisoner may also lead to faith--as one death row inmate discovered on Calvary.

Always remember . . .

... there are great men and women
of faith
on both sides of the prison wall.

1. Write the key verse from memory.

____

____

2. List and describe the common security levels.

____

____

3. Discuss the differences between jails and prisons.

____

____

4. What are some other facilities of confinement discussed in this chapter?

____

____

5. Discuss what you learned in this chapter regarding inmate typology.

____

____

____

____

6. How should you deal with inmates who maintain their innocence?

____

(Answers to self-tests are provided at the conclusion of the final chapter in this manual.)

CHAPTER ELEVEN
Dress And Safety Codes

KEY VERSE:

Let every soul be subject to the governing authorities. For there is no authority except from God, and the authorities that exist are appointed by God. (Romans 13:1)

OBJECTIVES:

Upon conclusion of this chapter you will be able to:

- Describe dress codes applicable for all penal institutions.
- Summarize safety codes applicable for all penal institutions.
- Give guidelines for surviving a hostage incident.

INTRODUCTION

Most penal institutions have specific dress and safety codes. Be sure to inquire about these, and ask for them in writing if they are available. In this chapter, you will learn general dress and safety codes applicable to all institutions. You will also learn how to survive a hostage incident, in the rare instance that one should ever occur.

APPROPRIATE ATTIRE

Each jail and prison usually has a dress code that applies to their specific institution. For example, some institutions prohibit volunteers and visitors from wearing colors that resemble inmate or guard uniforms. Be sure to ask about the rules for the specific institution you are visiting. Here are some general rules of appropriate attire applicable to all institutions:

-Do not wear tight, form fitting clothing.
-Do not wear low cut necklines.
-Avoid tee shirts with emblems and slogans as an outer garment.
-No gang-related attire.
-Do not wear see-through or revealing clothing.
-No shorts.

- For women:
> -Dresses or skirts should come below the knee.
> -Avoid attire that reveals underwear straps.
> (some institutions ban sleeveless dresses and blouses for this reason).

Generally speaking, wear attire that is appropriate in the business world. You are there on business for the King of Kings!

> "A good volunteer will follow every rule in the institution. The rule may seem stupid, but he is happy to submit himself to it. One volunteer can destroy an entire program by not obeying the rules." A Prison Chaplain

SAFETY CODES

Each jail and prison usually has a dress code that applies to their specific institution. Be sure to ask about the rules for the institution you are visiting. Adherence to the rules will insure that your Christian witness is valid and will make your ministry effective.   Learn and obey all the rules at your local institution.

Here are some general rules applicable to all institutions:

1. Leave the following at home or in your car: Purses, wallets, briefcases, money and non-essentials.
2. Always carry identification. Many institutions insist on your identification having a photo.
3. Be prepared to submit to a search at any time.
4. Meet and arrive together if you are coming to minister as a group. Some institutions will escort you to your destination.
5. Be sure to adhere to the dress code of the institution.
6. Always consult the chaplain or a staff member when in doubt. Do not assume anything!
7. If you are ministering in a group, keep your eyes on each other, especially while entering and exiting the institution. (Note: Men should keep ladies in view at male institutions and ladies do the same for men at female institutions.) Don't stray from the group.
8. Never run in the institution. Running usually indicates that someone is being chased or is chasing someone. It is usually perceived as a danger signal.
9. Learn your way around the institution. Do not enter any restricted areas. Always walk on the sidewalks. Do not take short cuts (they could lead to danger).

10.   Know emergency procedures. Some institutions have alarms in the meeting rooms or give personal alarms or whistles to volunteers. You are expected to obey an officer when an order, command, direction or instruction is given. This is for your protection and the security of the institution. If you can't be an asset during an emergency, get out of the way. In the event of an emergency situation that affects a significant portion of the inmate population at an institution, the visiting program and other activities may be suspended during the emergency.

11.   In the event of a medical emergency with an inmate, know the procedure for summoning medical aid.

12.   If a crime is committed. . .
      -Call for help immediately
      -Secure the crime scene.
      -Remain in control and calm others around you.

13.   Do not take any contraband items into an institution. These obviously include drugs, explosives, alcohol, and weapons. It also includes items that you might not think of--for example something like chewing gum which can be used as a mold to imprint keys or jam locks. Be sure to ask what is permissible to take in with you.

14.   Never take medications (legal drugs) into any institution. Do not enter the institution with your abilities impaired by medication.

15.   Never take cameras or tape recorders onto prison grounds without permission. Photos are considered a security risk if they fall into the wrong hands.

16.   Never leave your clothing (coats, sweaters, etc.) where it may be picked up and used by prisoners in an escape attempt.

17.   If you are given keys, keep them on you at all time. Do not lay them down anywhere! If you are responsible for closing up a room and locking it, be sure to search the room before doing so. Check store rooms, under desks, corners, bathrooms. Be sure it is empty.

18.   Officers assigned to entrances, exits, and gates are responsible for identifying you and for searching any car, package, purse, or briefcase that passes through. When the officer at the gate is processing a visitor or inmates, do not interrupt him.

19.   Do not take messages to or from inmates--verbal or written--outside the institution. Passing messages for prisoners to others outside could--unknowingly--be contributing to an escape attempt.

20.   Many institutions issue an identification badge or card to volunteers. Be sure to wear or carry this with you at all times on institutional grounds.

SURVIVING HOSTAGE SITUATIONS

Chances are remote--but if you are providing services in correctional institutions you must be alert to the possibility of being taken hostage. The following guidelines are used with permission of the American Correctional Association:

1.   Be cautious of heroics. Don't act foolishly.

2.   Be cooperative and obey hostage takers' demands without appearing either servile or antagonistic.
3.   Look for a protected place where you could hide if either authorities or inmates attempt to assault your location with force.
4.   Keep calm.
5.   Keep a low profile. Avoid the appearance of observing crimes that rioters commit. Look down or away. Avoid interfering with their discussions or activities.
6.   Do not make threats against hostage takers or give any indication that you would testify against them. If inmates are attempting to conceal their identities, make no indication that you recognize them.
7.   Be reluctant to give up your identification or clothes. Loss of these things is demoralizing. Inmates will use them for bargaining. Be especially resistant to exchanging clothes with an inmate. This could put you in much greater danger in case of an assault.
8.   As a result of the stress of the hostage situation, you may have difficulty retaining fluids. If it is possible and the hostage incident is lengthy, try to drink water and eat--even if you are not hungry.
9.   Do not say or do anything to arouse the hostility or suspicions of your captors. Act neutral and be a good listener if your captors want to talk. Be cautious about making suggestions to your captors as you may be held responsible if something you suggest goes wrong.
10.   Think of persuasive reasons the hostage takers should keep you and the other hostages alive and not harm you. Encourage them to let authorities know your whereabouts and condition. Suggest possible ways you or others may benefit your captors in negotiations that would free you.
11.   If you, as hostage, end up serving as negotiator between inmates and authorities, messages between the two groups should be conveyed accurately.
12.   If there is an assault to rescue and shots are fired, drop quickly to the floor and seek cover. Keep your hands on your head. When appropriate, identify yourself. Do not resist being apprehended until positive identification is made.
13.   Even though you must appear disinterested while being held hostage, observe all you can and make notes immediately after your release. All of these things will help in subsequent prosecution of the rioters.

Most important--in addition to the above practical guidelines--pray fervently and maintain your dependence on the Holy Spirit. Remember that nothing happens without God's permission. Therefore, keep in mind that "All things work together for good to them that love God" (Romans 8:28). You have nothing to fear. God will deliver you according to His will and time frame. If need be, He can send legions of angels to rescue you!

A final note: Please do not let this necessary discussion of safety codes and hostage-taking discourage you from entering the prison ministry. Your are in more danger on the highways of your city than going into a prison! Inmates have even been known to shield volunteers from rioters because they knew they really cared.

SELF TEST FOR CHAPTER ELEVEN

1. Write the key verse from memory.

____

____

2. Describe appropriate dress codes applicable for all penal institutions.

____

____

3. Summarize safety codes applicable for all penal institutions.

____

____

____

____

4. Summarize the guidelines given in this chapter for surviving a hostage incident.

____

____

____

5. Obtain a list of the dress and safety codes for the institution in which you are visiting or ministering. Insert these in the final section (Chapter Thirteen) of this manual which is designed for material unique to your specific institution.

(Answers to self-tests are provided at the conclusion of the final chapter in this manual).

CHAPTER TWELVE
Relating To Inmates

KEY VERSE:

. . .in humility correcting those who are in opposition, if God perhaps will grant them repentance, so that they may know the truth, and that they may come to their senses and escape the snare of the devil, having been taken captive by him to do his will. (2 Timothy 2:25-26)

OBJECTIVES:

Upon conclusion of this chapter you will be able to:

- Explain the first rule for relating with inmates.
- Summarize guidelines for relating to inmates.
- Define a "setup."
- Explain how a setup occurs.
- List three ways to avoid a setup.

INTRODUCTION

As a member of a prison ministry team, you represent Jesus Christ--not yourself. You are His ambassador. By your actions, words and/or dress, you can help or hinder the work of His Church behind bars.

Building relationships is not easy outside a prison and it isn't easy inside the prison. Some inmates may not be interested in spiritual matters. Some may completely reject you. Others may try to use you to further their own ends. It may help to recall Jesus' parable of the sower of seed and the four kinds of soil upon which the seed fell. Inmates, like everyone else, will fit into one of those categories. This chapter provides guidelines for successfully relating to inmates in a jail or prison setting.

THE FIRST RULE

The first rule in relating to inmates: Learn and follow all the rules specific to the institution where you are ministering: These include such things as visiting hours, who can and cannot come in, what can be brought in, where you can and cannot go, and the dress code. Chapter Eleven of this manual provides further information on matters pertaining to dress and safety codes which will not be repeated here. This chapter concerns relationships with inmates in personal contact and group situations.

GUIDELINES FOR RELATING TO INMATES

Inmates have had a great deal of frustration in their lives. Many have experienced repeated failure and are suspicious of any offer of assistance or guidance. Working with inmates cannot be reduced to a standard method. Much will be left to your good judgment.   The following are general guidelines, however, to use in relating to inmates:

-Don't establish a facade or create special status for yourself. Express yourself genuinely. Let the inmates know you are there out of genuine concern, because it is what the Lord will have you do. As a volunteer, you will be checked out and tested to see if you are real. Inmates will see what you are before they listen to what you say. They don't care how much you know until they know how much you care. Be honest. Inmates are very sensitive to hypocrisy and phonies.

-Learn as much of the prison-related language as possible, but be careful in using it. There may be subtle meanings of which you are unaware.

-Learn to present the salvation message in a clear and simple way. Big words such as "propitiation" and "atonement" don't mean much to the average inmate.

-Be sensitive during crisis periods which include immediately following arrest, the first few weeks in prison, prior to and right after a trial, when appeals are denied, and just prior to release. Holidays are also difficult periods.

-Mean what you say. Yes is yes, no is no. Be consistent and fair. Enforcing rules for some and relaxing them for others is inconsistent and unfair. It is also a form of over-familiarity.

-Be supportive, encouraging, friendly and firm. Be honest, objective, and disapproving when it is warranted. Be friendly, but not overly familiar.

-Respect is the key. You must respect the inmate's individuality and basic rights. Avoid prejudices and feelings of superiority. Respond to the inmate's needs and interests, not your own. Once you have earned the respect and trust of the inmate, he will be open to you.

-Never allow residents to manipulate you with over-dramatized stories of being falsely accused, unjustly incarcerated, or inhumanely treated. These are often used to arouse sympathy or manipulate you.   If you think the story is true--and in some cases they are-- inform the inmate of your intentions to share it with the chaplain and ask him to handle it.

-Never make inflammatory statements or careless remarks to staff or inmates about political groups, ethnic groups, other religious groups, prison staff, individual residents, or other prison ministry volunteers.

-Never assume an inmate is innocent or guilty and do not give legal counsel or advice. You are not a lawyer or judge.

-Never reveal personal details, if you are privy to them, about the lives of staff or other inmates.

-A good policy is to make only promises you know you can fulfill, and then as few of them as possible. When refusing a request explain why it is necessary and express your regrets.

-One of the best ways to avoid familiarity in a group setting is to address each member of the ministry team, as well as the inmates, as "brother" or "sister"--using first or last names. (This is not necessary in one-on-one visiting or corresponding with an inmate.)

-Do not routinely give out your home address or telephone number. Some institutions make it expensive for residents to make any phone calls, even local ones--and you are usually expected to pay the costs. If you do give out your number, establish how often you want to receive telephone calls.

-Never inquire as to why the resident is in prison. This could be embarrassing and you don't need to know why he/she is there to point him/her to Christ. Some inmates want to tell you about their case, and if so, it is all right to listen, encourage, and pray with them.

-Guard against over-familiarity--especially advances of a sexual nature. Your relationship with inmates--especially in a group setting--should be professional. Guard your emotions, especially if you are of the opposite sex. Expressions of affection will cause you to lose your volunteer status.   If an inmate makes an improper advance, handle it appropriately and then notify the chaplain or an administrator. At minimum, it is a test to see what your limits are.

-Never become involved in transacting personal business for residents.

-Do not be shocked or surprised by anything prisoners might say or how they say it.

-Never deliberately try to persuade prisoners to change their religious preference. You are there to share the Gospel--and it will do any changing that is necessary.

-Earn respect for yourself. Make it clear that you will not be manipulated. If a situation arises that you consider "borderline," check with prison officials to be sure of how it is to be handled.

-Expect hostility. An inmate, overwhelmed with problems, may confront you with hostility. At such times do not force conversation upon him and don't respond in a hostile, sarcastic, or anxious manner. Keep your composure, ignore the hostility, or withdraw for awhile. Chances are that the inmate will regain his composure. Always express unconditional love.

-Don't over-identify.   Don't take the inmate's problems upon yourself. They are not your problems. Over-identifying with inmates can bring about the we/they syndrome: "They are wrong about you."

-Don't expect thanks. You may not receive thanks or any show of gratitude from the inmate. He may feel it, but may not know how to express it. However, your effort will be appreciated and rewarded by God.

-You must set the limits. Some inmates will push you until you say to stop. How hard and far they push will depend on what you allow. Don't compromise.

-Don't panic if you find yourself alone with an inmate.

-Leave your personal problems at home. Inmates have enough problems of their own. They don't need to be burdened with yours.

-In a temperate and tolerant manner, always imply that you expect the correct attitude from inmates.

-Never show the slightest uncertainty as to the course of your action. You must be a leader in the strongest sense of the word, but also know and adhere to the limits of your authority.

-Never show that you have been angered by being profane, vulgar, or abusive in any manner.

-Express appreciation when behavior has been commendable--"You guys were great tonight--so attentive!"

-If prisoners request letters of recommendation to judges and other criminal justice authorities, inform them you will pass this request on to the chaplain for evaluation and possible action.

-Minister through personal counseling. Counseling provides a friendly and supportive relationship for the one seeking answers or a solution to a problem. This type of relationship can take place at the close of a worship service or Bible study session, when some prisoners may want to talk about what they heard or may have a problem to talk about. Most of the time they are not actually seeking solutions. They just want someone to listen and possibly be an encouraging and supportive friend.

-You may have access to information which is confidential. You are not to reveal this information to anyone not having an official right to it. The information is not to be used for your own advantage or benefit. You must be able to deal with an individual's spiritual problems as if you know nothing about his/her crimes. Keep issues discussed in counseling confidential unless they are a threat to institution security or if you learn that the inmate intends to do something drastic to himself or someone else. In these cases, don't tell him that you are going to report it, but report it.

-Be a good listener. You don't have to have answers to everything, but let them know that God does! If you think a prisoner needs formal counseling, encourage him/her to seek it through institutional channels.

-Don't make decisions for the inmate under any circumstances. Help them make their own decisions. This encourages responsibility for their own lives. Also, it prevents them from blaming you if things go wrong.

-Don't judge ideas or the inmate by appearance, vocabulary, or manner of speaking. View inmates as individuals. Don't make assumptions based upon generalities or stereotypes. Categorizing an inmate is unfair and dehumanizing.

-Don't interrupt immediately if you think a statement is wrong. Listen!

-Don't scold or interrogate them about their previous condition or what they may have done to be placed in here. Many already have a poor self-image.

-Be patient. The positive effects of your patience with the inmate may not have a decisive influence for awhile. Above all, don't ever become discouraged. Do your best, pray, and leave the results with God.

AVOIDING A SETUP

Quick sand is a patch of sand that looks like any other on the surface, but it is a dangerous patch of ground that can suck you under and cost your life. It is not as it appears on the surface. This is often true in relationships. People are not always as they seem to be on the surface. While not all inmates are steeped in criminal behavior, many of them are and because of that you must learn how to avoid a setup in the institutional environment.

WHAT IS A SETUP?

A "setup" is a situation where you are forced into compromising your own beliefs, standards, or institutional rules. You are forced or tricked into a compromising situation, and then taken advantage of by an inmate to receive favors or contraband like drugs, alcohol, etc.

HOW DOES A SETUP OCCUR?

A setup usually proceeds as follows:

Observation:

Inmates first observe your ability or inability to function under stress, your level of tolerance, whether or not you adhere to rules, and how effectively you will take command in a difficult situation.

Testing:

Before any conclusions can be drawn, inmates test their assumptions about you in minor ways. This may include such things as unauthorized requests for supplies and materials, asking for favors, circumventing rules, preying on sympathy, or attempting to engage you in intimate conversations.   If you yield in these "minor areas," then you are a prime candidate for a setup.

The Setup:

If you compromise minor rules or engage in intimate or inappropriate behavior, then an inmate sets you up by using this as a lever to get what they actually wanted all along. They will threaten to tell the administration about your minor infractions in the past or inform you that have actually been tricked into doing something illegal.   They use this as a lever to get what they want-- perhaps contraband like drugs or alcohol or other favors.

AVOIDING A SETUP:

You can avoid a setup by. . .

1.   Maintaining a professional attitude:

Professionalism is a word used to describe a specific attitude towards ministry in jails and prisons. Professionalism means that your standards and life-style should be better than the standards and life-style of the majority of people confined to prison. You are not being professional if you use inmate jargon or manipulate institutional rules as some inmates do.

2.   Avoiding familiarity:

We have stressed this repeatedly in this manual--you can maintain professionalism while still being friendly. Make a distinction between friendliness and familiarity. You are overly familiar if you allow the taking of license or liberties. Enforcing rules for one person but relaxing them for others is one example.   Engaging in intimate conversations or promising favors that are not within your jurisdiction to give are others.

3.   Refusing to violate rules under any circumstance:

A set-up always involves a previous infraction of rules. Refuse to violate rules under any circumstance.

4.   Immediately reporting a setup attempt:

If you are approached in this manner or you find yourself ensnared in a setup, immediately report it to the chaplain or administration.

SELF-TEST FOR CHAPTER TWELVE

1.   Write the key verse from memory.

____

2.   What is the first rule for properly relating with inmates?

____

3.   Summarize at least four of the guidelines for relating to inmates given in this chapter.

____

____

____

____

4.   What is a setup?

____

____

5.   How does a setup occur?

____

____

6.   List four ways to avoid a setup.

____

____

____

____

(Answers to self-tests are provided at the conclusion of the final chapter in this manual.)

CHAPTER THIRTEEN
Individualized Guidelines

This manual provides general guidelines for ministry applicable to most jail and prison settings. This final section is reserved for insertion of specific guidelines unique to the institution in which you will be ministering.

Here are some suggested items to insert in this section of the manual:

-An organizational chart for your prison ministry and/or that of the institution in which you will be ministering. (An organizational chart shows who is part of your ministry and who you are responsible to within the institution.)

-Rules for dress and safety specific to your institution.

-Guidelines on what you as a volunteer--or your ministry team--may bring or send into the institution where you minister: Bibles? Bible studies? Tracts? Cassette tapes? Videos?

-Specific guidelines for visiting inmates, including visitation days and hours and what can and cannot be brought or sent in.

-Guidelines for corresponding with inmates and items that can be sent through the mail.

-A map of the institution.

-Handouts from in-service training offered by the institution.

-Referral lists of local organizations or ministries that assist paroling inmates with housing, jobs, clothing, finances, etc.

-If you are a chaplain or a volunteer coordinator and have developed training materials unique to your institution, insert these materials in this section.

-If you are a Bible college instructor, insert your lecture notes and handouts in this section.

CONCLUSION

. . . but the Word of God is not bound. (2 Timothy 2:9)

Jesus is in your local jail. He is doing time in prison . . .

> **"Then the righteous will answer Him, saying, `Lord, when did we see You. . .
> in prison, and come to You?' And the King will answer and say to them,
> `Assuredly, I say to you, inasmuch as you did it to one of the least of these My
> brethren, you did it to Me.'" (Matthew 25:37-40)**

From a spiritual standpoint, there is no value that can be placed on the soul of a man, woman, or young person:

> **"For what profit is it to a man if he gains the whole world, and loses his own
> soul? Or what will a man give in exchange for his soul?" (Matthew 16:26)**

From a purely financial standpoint, every person kept out of prison saves thousands of dollars a year in direct costs of incarceration. This doesn't include the social service expenses for their families provided by some governments, nor does it calculate the tremendous human costs to the family or economic contributions the prisoner would make if gainfully employed.

By accepting the mandate for jail and prison ministries--by marching fearlessly past the rows of razor wire and armed guard posts--you are going into the very depths of hell to mine precious gems for the Lord.

Oh yes--there will be some who do not receive your message. There will be others who will profess, but not really possess. There will be some who return back to their old ways. But remember . . .

> -God started with a man and woman with a perfect heritage who lived in a perfect environment, and both of them failed.
>
> -When Jesus revealed that He must suffer, many disciples ceased to follow Him--they were not willing to pay the cost.
>
> -In His final hours, His remaining disciples fled, one denied Him, and one betrayed Him--yet several of these men fulfilled the great challenge of taking the Gospel to the nations of the world.

Do not measure the worth of jail and prison ministries by your failures. Measure its worth by your successes. You are part of a world-wide network that is changing the world--One jail and prison at a time, one person at a time.

There are many challenges to jail and prison ministry, but there are also tremendous rewards. Volunteers often start working with inmates and ex-offenders thinking, "I'll go into this dark place and take the love of God." Very often, they come out testifying, "I got more than I gave."

By accepting the mandate of jail and prison ministry you become part of an exciting team--a world-wide network of volunteers who are gathering up jewels for the Master.

> **"They shall be Mine," says the LORD of hosts, "On the day that I make them My jewels. . .And I will spare them as a man spares his own son who serves him." (Malachi 3:17)**

Continue to raise up spiritual sons and daughters until the Master returns:
-Don't ever be discouraged.
-Don't ever lose the vision.
-Don't ever give up on an inmate.
-Don't ever quit.

> **"Lift up your eyes all around, and see: they all gather together, they come to you; your sons shall come from afar, and your daughters shall be nursed at your side." (Isaiah 60:4)**

Life. . .In The Shadow Of Death

It is Easter Sunday, and a bright sun breaks through the clouds illuminating our Central California valley town with its warmth. This is the day to celebrate life, but our Easter observance will take us into the very shadows of death. We invite you to come along--it is a celebration of life in Jesus that you won't soon forget.

We enter the Central California Women's Facility through multiple gates and check points. This prison houses close to 4,000 inmates at the present time, including high security, death row prisoners.   The place where we celebrate the resurrection is in the very shadow of death, just as the empty tomb in Jerusalem is in the shadow of Golgotha's Hill. We are surrounded by two rows of razor wire with a deadly electrified fence running between them. Above us looms the armed guard towers and across the main yard in the distance rises the imposing image of California's death row for women.

Our service is not scheduled to begin until noon, but at 10: 30 a.m., women are already lining up. By 11 a.m., we open the chapel and we are immediately packed out. There are women lining the walls and the platform, standing at the back, and outside peering through the windows. Many of the women are tattooed, rather tough-looking, and some are overtly lesbian. Yet they have come here today to receive the message of life.

When we open the service, the room literally explodes with excitement. As we join together in praise and worship, one inmate plays the piano, another the bongo drums, a third maintains rhythm on a full set of drums. Add several tambourines and maracas to this, an integrated choir with a soul beat, and the most enthusiastic singing you can imagine!

As an inmate concludes the strains of a solo entitled "*The Blood*," a hush falls upon our rather diverse audience. We share a message regarding the death and resurrection of Jesus Christ entitled "*Four Gardens Of God*." From the Garden of Eden where blood was shed for Adam and Eve, we travel through the pages of God's Word to the Garden of Gethsemane where Jesus sweat great drops of blood, on to the garden at the feet of Golgotha's Hill where the blood flowed from the cross. We then focus on the garden of our hearts, where the blood of Jesus must also flow for sin.   As we call for commitments, hands are lifted all over the room and the miracle occurs: Spiritual life replaces spiritual death. You can literally feel the transformation and see it on the faces of the women.

As we look out over this packed room, we think of other inmates who have sat in these same seats over the years we have ministered at this prison and who are now paroled back to the free world. There is Debra, who received her B.A. in Christian education and is married and active in a local church. There is Irene, soon to receive her B.A., a member of the honor society and president of her school's business club. There is Rosie, now employed as a nurse, reunited with her children.

We have often been asked, "Why do you go to that prison and waste time on those people? Don't you know that many of them will just return to the institution again and again? Do you really think you can change them?" Our answer is, "No, <u>we</u> cannot change them. But the program we run has a 100% success rate when students incorporate its truths into their lives.   Our guarantee is recorded in Joshua 1:8:

> *"This book of the law shall not depart from your mouth, but you shall mediate in it day and night,*
> *that you may observe to do according to all that is written in it.*
> *For then you will make your way prosperous, and then you will have good success."*

APPENDIX ONE
Dictionary

You do not need to know inmate slang to conduct jail and prison ministry, but some basic terminology used frequently in prisons is helpful. The following terms are common in prisons throughout the United States.

> *Note: If you are preparing this manual for use in another country, you may want to remove this section and substitute one more appropriate to your institution.*

Ad Seg: Administrative Segregation. Placement in a controlled unit for the safety and security of the institution. Also called the "hole."

All day: A life sentence, as in "He's doing all day . . ."

Badge: A guard, correctional officer.

Banger: A knife. Also called a burner or a shank.

Beef: A disciplinary charge, as to "catch a beef."

Big House: Prison.

Big Jab: Lethal injection. Also called the "needle."

Blanket party: Throwing a blanket over a despised prisoner, so he or she can't identify an attacker.

Blind: Area where correctional officers cannot see.

Books: Trust fund account. All money received by a prisoner is placed into a trust account and may be withdrawn for canteen purchases, special orders, postage, and other expenses.

Box: A carton of cigarettes.

Bull: Guard.

Bunkie: The person with whom a prisoner shares a double bunk bed.

C-file: The central file. The critical information maintained on each prisoner.

Call: Time for specified events -- e.g., mail call or sick call. May be known in some jurisdictions as a call out.

Camp: Minimum security facilities for firefighting and conservation work.

Cellie: Cell mate.

Chain: Used when an inmate is transferred to another unit. "He left out on the chain yesterday."

Chrono: Informational notes by prison officials documenting classification decisions, minor disciplinary offenses, medical orders, and just about everything else that might be recorded on a prisoner.

Commissary: Prison "store" for buying stamps, toiletries, cigarettes, and other items.

Count: The institutional count, repeated at different times in the day. Everything stops while prison staff make sure no one is missing.

Date: The release date.

Ducat: Prison passes for movement in the institution. Assignments for jobs, cell changes, sick-call, and other prison programs. Trust fund withdrawals for canteen draws.

Fish: A new inmate.

Fish Line: A line used to pull items from one cell to another.

Fog line: When the fog is too thick for staff to keep a close watch, "fog line" will be called and prisoners will be restricted to their cells or unit.

Good Time: Credits earned toward one's sentence.

Hard Time: Serving a sentence the difficult way.

Hit: A planned murder or stabbing.

Hole: Solitary confinement, segregation, disciplinary detention cells.

Homeboy: Another prisoner from one's hometown or neighborhood.

Hooch: Homemade (or cell made) alcohol

Ink: Tattoos.

Inside: Behind the walls.

Jacket: An inmate's prison record.

Jail: A county facility for pretrial detainees or prisoners serving short terms.

Jailhouse Lawyer: A prisoner who assist others in filing legal actions.

Kite: Notes or letters. Any message passed to a prisoner.

Lifer: A prisoner serving a life sentence.

Lock down: An individual inmate, a specific housing unit, or the entire prison may be locked down when there is a threat to security, count doesn't clear, or someone is missing.

Lock Up Unit: Segregated unit; the adjustment center; disciplinary detention.

L.W.O.P.: Life Without Possibility of Parole.

Mainline: Also called "general population"--as distinct from those housed on death row or in special housing units.

Make Paper: Make parole.

Man: Guard or authority -- "The Man."

Man Walking: A signal that a guard is coming.

MTA: Medical technician.

Packing: A prisoner who is carrying a weapon or drugs for sale.

PC: Protective custody.

PHU: Protective Housing Unit. Unit assigned to prisoners who cannot program anywhere else in the system and meet certain criteria.

PIA: Prison Industry Authority.

Priors: Previous prison terms, enhancing one's sentence or affecting the classification score.

Seg: Segregation (isolated or disciplinary unit).

Shakedown: A search of a cell or work area.

Shank: Handmade prison weapon--generally a stabbing instrument. Also called a shiv or a piece.

Short-timer: An inmate who will soon be released.

SHU: Security Housing Unit. Segregation, the Hole.

Snitch: An informant. One who has given up names or activities.

Stinger: Appliance used to heat water, which may be created by attaching live electrical wires to a metal plate. Permitted in some prisons.

Street: The outside world, as in "on the street."

Yard: The exercise area. In segregation, the yard may be nothing more than a concrete "dog run" with no equipment. Other units may have a basketball court, recreation equipment, or grassy areas.

APPENDIX TWO
Scriptures Related To Prisoners

This appendix will enable you to study references that are made to prisoners/prisons in the Bible.

Genesis 39:11-41:14: Joseph's imprisonment.

Genesis 42:15-20: Joseph imprisons his brothers.

Genesis 45:4-8: Joseph reveals himself to his brothers.

Numbers 21:1: The Israelites are imprisoned.

Judges 16:21-25: Samson is blinded and imprisoned.

1 Kings 22:27: Micaiah is imprisoned because of his prophetic ministry.

2 Kings 17:4: Hoshea, king of Israel, is imprisoned by the king of Assyria for being a traitor.

2 Kings 24:10-12: King Jehoiachin of Israel is taken prisoner by Nebuchadnezzar.

2 Kings 25:27-30: Jehoiachin is released from prison by the new king of Babylon.

2 Chronicles 16:7-10: Hanani is imprisoned by Asa, King of Judah, for giving a prophesy.

2 Chronicles 18:26: Micaiah is imprisoned by Ahab, king of Israel, because of his prophecy.

Psalm 69:33: The Lord does not despise prisoners.

Psalm 79:11 and 102:20: A request for the Lord to preserve those condemned to die.

Psalm 146:7: The Lord sets prisoners free.

Isaiah 14:17: Satan does not allow his captives to go home.

Isaiah 24:21-22: The kings of the earth are imprisoned.

Isaiah 42:7: The prophecy of Jesus coming to free the captives in prison.

Isaiah 49:9: In the day of salvation, the Lord will tell captives and those in darkness to be free.

Isaiah 53:8: Jesus' imprisonment foretold.

Isaiah 61:1: The proclamation of the Lord's anointed to announce freedom for prisoners.

Jeremiah 32:1-2: Jeremiah imprisoned in Judah.

Jeremiah 32:6-15: Jeremiah buys a field while in prison.

Jeremiah chapter 33: The Lord speaks to Jeremiah while he is in prison.

Jeremiah 36:5: Jeremiah dictates the Lord's Word to Baruch during his imprisonment.

Jeremiah 36:26: Jehoiakim tries to have Jeremiah arrested.

Jeremiah 37:4-38:13: Falsely accused of desertion, the prophet Jeremiah is beaten and imprisoned.

Jeremiah 38:28: Jeremiah continues his imprisonment until Jerusalem is captured.

Jeremiah 40:1-4: Jeremiah is freed by the imperial guard.

Jeremiah 52:11: Zedekiah, king of Jerusalem, is blinded and imprisoned for life by the king of Babylon.

Jeremiah 52:31-34: Jehoiachin, King of Judah, is released from prison by the king of Babylon.

Lamentations 3:34: God does not willingly afflict prisoners.

Lamentations 3:53-55: Jeremiah pleads with God during his imprisonment.

Daniel 3:1-28: Shadrach, Meshach, and Abednego are thrown into a fiery furnace and rescued by God.

Daniel 6:16-24: Daniel is incarcerated in the lion's den and is rescued by the Lord.

Zechariah 9:11-12: God's promise to deliver prisoners.

Matthew 4:12;11:2;14:3,10; Mark 1:4,6:17,27; Luke 3:20: John the Baptist is imprisoned and executed.

Matthew 5:25-26: It is best to make peace with an adversary who is taking you to court. Otherwise, a prison term may be forthcoming.

Matthew 18:30: The unmerciful servant puts a man who owes him money into jail.

Matthew 25:35,39,44: Jesus states that people who minister to those in prison are ministering to Him and that people who neglect to do so have neglected to minister to Him.

Matthew 27:15-21; Mark 15:6; Luke 23:19,25: Barabbas is released from prison instead of Jesus.

Luke 4:18: Jesus states His calling, which is the fulfillment of Isaiah 61:1-3 and includes ministry to prisoners.

Luke 12:58-59: Be reconciled to your adversary so you can escape imprisonment.

Luke 21:12-13: Jesus tells His disciples that they will be imprisoned because of His name and that this will result in their being witnesses.

Luke 22:33: Peter declares he is ready to follow Jesus to prison and death.

Luke 23:19,25: The release of Barabbas at the request of the people.

Matthew 27; Mark 15; Luke 23; John 19: Jesus is taken captive and dies for the sins of the world.

Acts 4:3: Peter and John are imprisoned.

Acts 5:18-23: The apostles are imprisoned and then freed by an angel of the Lord.

Acts 5:40: The apostles are punished for preaching in the name of Jesus.

Acts 7:54-60: Stephen, a believer, is executed for his faith.

Acts 8:3; 9:2,14,21: Saul is persecuting and incarcerating Christians prior to his conversion to Christ.

Acts 12:1-2: James, the brother of John, is put to death by Herod.

Acts 12:3-17: Peter is imprisoned and then freed by an angel of the Lord.

Acts 12:18-19: Herod puts to death those who had been guarding Peter.

Acts 14:19: Paul is stoned by the crowd and assumed dead.

Acts 16:25-39: Paul and Silas are beaten and imprisoned. An earthquake occurs, the prison doors open, and their chains are loosed. The jailer and his family are saved and Paul and Silas are freed by the magistrates.

Acts 20:22-24: Paul predicts his future imprisonment in Jerusalem.

Acts 21:11: Agabus, a prophet, confirms that Paul will be imprisoned in Jerusalem.

Acts 21:30-35: A crowd in Jerusalem seizes Paul with the intention to kill him. Paul is saved by Roman soldiers.

Acts 22:24-29: Paul testifies that he previously persecuted and imprisoned Christians.

Acts 23:1-35: Paul speaks before the Sanhedrin and is imprisoned.

Acts chapter 24: Paul's trial before Felix and his appeal to Ceasar.

Acts chapter 25: Paul's trial before Festus.

Acts chapter 26: Paul's trial before Agrippa.

Acts chapter 27:1-28:15: Paul's trip to Rome while in the custody of Roman soldiers.

Acts 28:17-20: Paul talks about his imprisonment.

Acts 28:16: Paul is allowed to live under house arrest with a guard to watch him.

2 Corinthians 11:23: Paul talks about his imprisonments and the hardships he has suffered for Christ.

Ephesians 3:1; 4:1: Paul states that he is a prisoner of Christ.

Ephesians 6:20: Paul states that he is an ambassador in chains.

Philippians 1:11-18: Paul states that his imprisonment has advanced the cause of Christ.

Colossians 4:10: Aristarchus is a fellow prisoner of Paul.

2 Timothy 1:8: Paul asks that people not be ashamed of his incarceration for the cause of Christ.

2 Timothy 1:16-17: Paul blesses Onesiphorus for his ministry to him in prison.

2 Timothy 2:9: Paul says that although he is bound, the Word of God is not bound.

2 Timothy 4:16-17: The Lord stood by Paul's side when everyone else deserted him because of his imprisonment.

Philemon 1:9-10: Paul requests mercy for Onesimus who was saved in prison.

Philemon 1:23: Epaphras is a fellow-prisoner of Paul.

Hebrews 13:3: Remember those in prison as if you were their fellow-prisoners.

1 Peter 3:19: Christ ministers to those in prison.

2 Peter 2:4: God imprisoned the angels who revolted against Him.

Jude 1:6: God imprisoned the angels who revolted against Him.

Revelation 2:10: The devil will imprison believers.

Revelation 2:13: Antipas, God's faithful witness, is put to death.

Revelation 20:7: Satan is released from prison for a short time before his final incarceration in the lake of fire.

ANSWERS TO SELF-TESTS

CHAPTER ONE:

1.   . . . I was in prison, and you came to me. (Matthew 25:36)

2.   The main reference for the scriptural mandate for prison ministry is Matthew 25:31-40.

3.   Jesus is our greatest Biblical example for prison ministry.

4.   Eight reasons why believers should be involved in prison ministry are:

   1. Prison ministry has a direct Scriptural mandate (Matthew 25:39-40).
   2. We should follow the example Christ set by ministering to prisoners.
   3. Prisons meet the criteria of any mission field: Lost people and a need for laborers.
   4. God is not willing that any should perish
   5. Chaplains cannot minister to more than a small percentage of inmates in their care.
   6. Many jails and prisons have no professional chaplains and no religious services.
   7. For every person incarcerated, there are three to five other people affected.
   8. False religions and cults are reaching out to prisoners. We must get there first with the Gospel of Jesus Christ!

5.   The spiritual goals of jail and prison ministry include the following:

   -To share the unconditional love of God.
   -To present the Gospel of Jesus Christ in such a way that inmates will embrace it and receive Christ as Savior.
   -To disciple new believers in the Word and teach them how to study the Bible.
   -To demonstrate the power of prayer and teach them to pray.
   -To lead inmates to experience the life-changing power of God that will free them from guilt, shame, negative emotions, and addictions.
   -To minister to inmates' families.

6.   The social goals of jail and prison ministry include the following:
   -To help the inmate function more positively within the prison environment.
   -To provide a link between the community and persons confined in correctional institutions
   -To prepare residents for re-entry into society (physically, mentally, morally and spiritually).
   -To assist inmates families in practical ways.
   -To provide post-prison assistance in practical ways.

7.	The Gospel offers inmates:

-Forgiveness from sin.
-A chance to say "I'm sorry."
-Release from guilt and shame.
-Acceptance.
-New values and perspectives.
-Strategies for coping with difficult situations and negative emotions
-Basics for true honest relationships.
-Life abundant through Jesus Christ.
-A new purpose for living.
-Eternal life.

CHAPTER TWO:

1.	. . . be an example to the believers in word, in conduct, in love, in spirit, in faith, in purity. (1 Timothy 4:12)

2.	Check your summary against the list of spiritual qualifications for a prison ministry volunteer discussed in this chapter.

3.	Four areas of preparation vital to effective prison ministry are:
	1. Prepare in prayer.
	2. Prepare in the Word.
	3. Prepare in your specific anointing.
	4. Prepare for the specific institution.

CHAPTER THREE:

1.	But this is a people robbed and plundered; all of them are snared in holes, and they are hidden in prison houses; they are for prey, and no one delivers; for plunder, and no one says, "Restore!" (Isaiah 42:22)

2.	Compare your summary to the steps for starting a prison ministry discussed in this chapter.

3.   The various ministries which you might provide in an institution include:

>-Conducting church services.
>-Substituting for the chaplain.
>-Providing special musical or dramatic programs.
>-Conducting Bible studies.
>-Teaching classes.
>-Conducting a Christian group for those with addictions.
>-Distributing literature and Bibles.
>-Hosting a Christian film night.
>-Providing individualized services. . .
>>-Providing Bible correspondence courses.
>>-Matching inmates with Christian visitors.
>>-Matching inmates with Christians to write to them.
>>-Providing referral information for families.
>>-Referring inmates to post-prison release programs.

4.   Some ways to recruit volunteers include:
>-Put a notice in church bulletins.
>-Make announcement in church services.
>-Recruit at small group meetings.
>-Prepare posters and place them in strategic locations in the church.
>-Plan a "Prison Ministry Day."

5.   Compare your summary of training volunteers to the discussion in this chapter.

CHAPTER FOUR:

1.   These things I have written to you who believe in the name of the Son of God, that you may know that you have eternal life, and that you may continue to believe in the name of the Son of God. (1 John 5:13)

2.   Two important things to do when you want to start corresponding with an inmate are:
>-Contact the proper authorities at the institution.
>-Obtain a list of the rules for corresponding with inmates at that specific prison.

3.   Compare your summary to the guidelines for corresponding with inmates discussed in this chapter.

CHAPTER FIVE:

1. Remember the prisoners as if chained with them--those who are mistreated--since you yourselves are in the body also. (Hebrews 13:3)

2. Personal visitation is an important ministry because:
     -Every soul is valuable to God.
     -Many inmates will not attend religious services.
     -Many inmates have never experienced true, Godly, unconditional friendship.
     -It is easier to open up in a personal rather than group setting.
     -You become a bridge back into society for the inmate.
     -You will not only be a blessing, but you will be blessed by a true friendship with an inmate.

3. You can get involved in one-on-one visitation with inmates by the following ways:
     -Inquire about the visitation program at the jail or prison where you want to volunteer.
     ~∫f the institution does not have an organized program for matching inmates and visitors, ask the chaplain or administrator to match you with an inmate.
     -People who are ministering inside the prison on a group basis in religious programs are also a good source.
     -If possible, exchange a few letters with the inmate prior to your first visit.

4. Compare your summary to the guidelines given in this chapter for visiting individually with an inmate.

CHAPTER SIX:

1. But when He saw the multitudes, He was moved with compassion for them, because they were weary and scattered, like sheep having no shepherd. (Matthew 9:36)

2. Some types of group meetings that can be conducted in jails and prisons include:
     -Worship services
     -Bible studies
     -Music classes
     -Musical and dramatic presentations
     -Christian writing
     -Small groups offering a Christian approach to addiction and/or emotional problems
     -Parenting classes
     -Bible college courses
     -Discipleship classes for new believers

3.   Compare your summary for each area to the guidelines given in this chapter.

CHAPTER SEVEN:

1.   ". . . and in you all the families of the earth shall be blessed." (Genesis 12:3)

2.   An inmate's family is often in crisis because when a family member is arrested it creates great anxiety, fear, and uncertainty. The family is split apart. Children face shame and loss when a parent is in prison.

3.   You can minister to inmate's families through the following ways:
        -Transportation and hospitality
        -Information
        -Social services
        -Employment
        -Housing, food, clothing, and finances
        -Counseling
        -Presents on special occasions
        -A church home

4.   Two important things you must do before contacting an inmate's family are:
        1.   Check with the chaplain or administration at the jail or prison where you are ministering.
        2.   Obtain written permission from the inmate so the family and institution knows you have his/her approval.

5.   Compare your summary to the guidelines given in this chapter for ministering to inmate's families.

CHAPTER EIGHT:

1.   Let the sighing of the prisoner come before thee; according to the greatness of thy power preserve thou those that are appointed to die. (Psalms 79:11)

2.   Compare your summary to the suggestions given in this chapter on how to start a death row ministry.

3.   Compare your discussion to the guidelines given in this chapter for ministering to death row inmates.

4.	You can help a death row inmate face death in the following ways:

-Is there someone they need to forgive? Guide them in the process.

-Are there those to whom he needs to apologize and seek forgiveness--victims, their families, his own family or friends?

-If they have young children, encourage them to write a special letter to the child to be given to them when they are older.

-Do they have any practical business matters that need to be concluded?

-Discuss death openly, and the fact that as a believer, there is nothing to fear.

-Help them focus on eternity and the tremendous things that await in Heaven.

-If they ask you to be present at their death to provide spiritual support, do so if the prison permits it.

CHAPTER NINE:

1.	. . .To open blind eyes, *to bring out the prisoners from the prison*, and them that sit in darkness out of the prison house. (Isaiah 42:7)

2.	Some of common needs of ex-offenders are:

-He needs to be accepted in a local church that is nurturing and supportive so he can develop spiritually.
-He needs housing, food, and clothing.
-He needs vocational training and/or a job.
-He may need financial counseling.
-Family counseling is important if he is trying to reunite his family.
-He may need additional personal counseling for addictions like drugs and alcohol.
-If he has been incarcerated for a long time, he may need assistance with even simple decisions.
-He needs a strong support network of friends who will love and accept him, pray for and with him, and help him work through problems.

3.	Post-prison ministries include:
		-A Christian "half way house"
		-The local rescue mission
		-Government or privately operated programs
		-Church based programs
		-Christian colleges and Bible schools

4.	The steps for starting a post-prison ministry are:
		-Step One: Pray
		-Step Two: Consult your spiritual leader
		-Step Three: Do an analysis
		-Step Four: Visit a similar ministry
		-Step Five: Determine organizational issues
			-Funding
			-Facilities
			-Staffing

5.	The three questions that should determine your role in post-prison ministry are:
	1.		What is permitted by the institution in which you minister?
	2.		Where are you most effective?
	3.		What are your time and energy limitations?

CHAPTER TEN:

1.	The spirit of the Lord God is upon me; because the Lord hath anointed me to preach good tidings unto the meek; he hath sent me to bind up the brokenhearted, to proclaim liberty to the captives, and the opening of the prison to them that are bound. . . (Isaiah 61:1)

2.	The common security levels are maximum, medium, minimum.

3.	Prison inmates have been tried and convicted. Jail is usually the entry point for all prisoners. Many jail inmates haven't been convicted of anything yet. Prison population is relatively stable. Jail population is very transient. Some prisons have at least a minimum of facilities and programs for counseling and rehabilitation, but most jails have few or none. Prisons usually have better facilities for group meetings such as church services and group Bible studies. The physical, emotional, and psychological conditions of jail inmates are different from and less favorable than those in prisons.

4.   Some other facilities of confinement discussed in this chapter are:
        -Work release centers
        -Halfway house
        -Road camp, fire camp, forestry camp, or work farm
        -Detention, juvenile hall, or reformatory

5.   Compare your summary to the discussion on inmate typology in this chapter.

CHAPTER ELEVEN:

1.   Let every soul be subject to the governing authorities. For there is no authority
        except from God, and the authorities that exist are appointed by God.
        (Romans 13:1)

2.   Compare your answer to the discussion on appropriate dress codes in this chapter.

3.   Compare your summary of safety codes to the discussion in this chapter.

4.   Compare your summary to the guidelines given in this chapter for surviving a hostage
        incident.

5.   Be sure to obtain a list of the dress and safety codes for the institution in which you are
        visiting or ministering. Insert these in the final section (Chapter Thirteen) of this manual
        which is designed for material unique to your specific institution.

CHAPTER TWELVE:

1.   . . .in humility correcting those who are in opposition, if God perhaps will grant
        them repentance, so that they may know the truth, and that they may come to their
        senses and escape the snare of the devil, having been taken captive by him to do
        his will. (2 Timothy 2:25-26)

2.   The first rule for properly relating with inmates is learn and follow the rules.

3.   Compare your summary to the guidelines for relating to inmates given in this chapter.

4.   A setup is a situation where you are forced into compromising your own beliefs,
        standards, or institutional rules. You are forced or tricked into a compromising situation,
        and then taken advantage of by an inmate to receive favors or contraband like drugs,
        alcohol, etc.

5.   A setup usually proceeds as follows:

Observation: Inmates first observe your ability or inability to function under stress, your level of tolerance, whether or not you adhere to rules, and how effectively you will take command in a difficult situation.

Testing: Before any conclusions can be drawn, inmates test their assumptions about you by such things as unauthorized requests for supplies and materials, asking for favors, circumventing rules, preying on sympathy, or attempting to engage you in intimate conversations.   If you yield in these "minor areas," then you are a prime candidate for a setup.

The Setup: If you compromise minor rules or engage in intimate or inappropriate behavior, then an inmate sets you up by using this as a lever to get what they actually wanted all along.

6.	You can avoid a setup by:

	1. Maintaining a professional attitude
	2. Avoiding familiarity
	3. Refusing to violate rules under any circumstance
	4. Immediately reporting a setup attempt

CHAPTER THIRTEEN:

Individualized chapter. No self-test.